Journey to Peace and Healing

a reflective journal

DAWN MICHELE JACKSON

*Debbie —
Thank you for being a part of my journey!
Love, Dawn ♡*

Journey to Peace and Healing

Copyright © 2023 by Dawn Michele Jackson

All rights reserved. No part of this publication may be reproduced, distributed, or transmitted in any form or by any means, including photocopying, recording, or other electronic or mechanical methods, without the prior written permission of the publisher, except in the case of brief quotations embodied in critical reviews and certain other noncommercial uses permitted by copyright law.

ISBN: 979-8-9868507-4-0

Book Design by Transcendent Publishing

Cover photo by Austin James Jackson Photography
www.austinjamesjackson.com

Editing by Lori Lynn

The content of this book is for informational purposes only and is not intended to diagnose, treat, cure, or prevent any condition or disease. You understand that this book is not intended as a substitute for consultation with a licensed practitioner. Please consult with your own physician or healthcare specialist regarding any physical or mental health issues you are experiencing. The use of this book implies your acceptance of this disclaimer.

Printed in the United States of America.

*For those who choose peace and healing despite the
mountains you may climb on your journey,
this is for you. May you find comfort in these words
and know you are not alone.*

*For those who choose peace and healing despite the
mountains you may climb on your journey,
this is for you. May you find comfort in these words
and know you are not alone.*

Contents

Introduction vii

Who Are You? 1

Feeling Lost 9

The Grief Within 15

Feel, Heal, Reveal 27

Fear 33

The Power of the Mind 41

Releasing 49

Transition 55

The Power of "No" 61

Boundaries 69

Going Within 75

Rest 83

Honoring Our Relationships 91

Choosing Vulnerability 97

Being Present 103

Nurture Your Soul In Nature 109

Nurture Your Body with Nutrients 115

Healing Power of Animals 123

Choices 129

Grace	135
Accepting Your Present Reality	141
Solitude	147
Have Faith	153
Gratitude	159
Find the Gift	167
Love without Measure	173
Be the Change	179
Believe In You	185
Be the Light	191
Final Thoughts	197
Acknowledgments	199
About the Author	201
How to Get More Help	203

Introduction

As I sat on the couch, under the weight of loss and grief, I remember hearing, "all struggle in life is a gift." At that moment, I was in shock. I wanted to throw something at the person who expressed those words to me. How could a divorce at thirty years old be a "gift" in my life? How could the extreme heartache and feelings of failure I was experiencing lead to something wonderful?

All my hopes, dreams, and expectations went out the door. I was the mother of a three-year-old, a nurse working part time, and I owned a home. This was not how my life was "supposed" to go. Why was this happening to me? There were so many unanswered questions, and for days I barely functioned while spending most of my time in tears. Questions were running through my head: *Would I be able to keep my home? How would this affect my child? What will tomorrow look like?* I was devastated, and that certainly didn't feel like a gift.

I didn't realize until years later that those words spoken to me so long ago—the ones about the gift in struggle—were some of the wisest words I would ever hear. For it was in that struggle that I found myself. And it wasn't only the struggle of divorce, it was every struggle I've experienced in my life. Each one of them pushed me to deeper healing and exploration of who I really am as a person.

Growing up with alcoholism in my family, I was used to chaos. It felt normal to me. Unfortunately, it took me a long time to realize that peace does not come in the midst of chaos. Peace comes with healing. And at thirty years old, the only thing I wanted was my life back as I knew it because that would "fix" everything. However, my life wasn't meant to go back to what it previously looked like, and for that I am now extremely grateful.

The same person who imparted the wisdom behind the gift of struggle also helped me realize that after my divorce, I had absolutely no idea who I was or even what I enjoyed doing. Sadly, all I knew was that I was a mother, a wife, and a nurse. End of story.

No, that was definitely not the end of my story—although I had no idea all that life had in store for me!

It was after watching the movie *Dragonfly* and then seeing a commercial for a humanitarian organization that I realized it was time to focus on something besides my ongoing grief. I couldn't seem to help myself at that time, so I chose to put my energy into focusing on others. I had a calling deep in my soul, and that calling was to help someone other than myself.

Less than a year after my divorce, I found my introverted self taking part in a plastic surgery mission to Mexico. As I boarded the plane to Oaxaca, I realized that I would be meeting a group of individuals who knew nothing about me besides my medical background, so I could be whomever I chose to be. When the plane took flight, I thought, *I can reinvent myself.* I felt free for the first time in a long time, maybe in my whole life. To my new friends, I wasn't a grieving ex-wife who was now a single mother. I was a woman who chose to set off on an adventure by herself to a foreign country in hopes of giving others a gift. What I didn't realize is I would be receiving as much of a gift, if not more, than

INTRODUCTION

I provided to my young patients. My world would be forever transformed, which would start my own personal journey of healing.

As I sit here sharing my story, I find myself reflecting not only on this life experience but also all the struggles before and after that have been gifts to me. It's not that I could see the gift in the pain, heartache, and struggle at the time. It's that I can look back now and smile, knowing the universe has always been on my side, rooting for me to become the best possible version of myself.

I share this story and others as a story of hope, a story for healing. I share from my heart so that others know they are not alone and that they also know there is a way out. One of the hardest things is to feel that nobody understands what we are going through. The truth is that every person has a different experience, thoughts and feelings, even if the situation looks similar. But we can relate to one another. We can support each other through the roughest of times and give hope for a better tomorrow. We can always find peace again.

Writing for me has been a way to share my stories and the wisdom I've gained through my life experiences. If one person finds comfort or connection in my words, I've lived my purpose. If even one individual's life is impacted by my story, it will continue to ripple out into other lives and create a wave of change in our world.

Earlier in life, I thought that if I was able to heal something painful using a certain modality, then it would work for every heartache in my life. What I soon came to realize is that different circumstances and different time periods may require a completely new set of spiritual tools. The tool box keeps getting bigger and still does to this day as I navigate life. And by navigating life, I don't only speak of the hard times. I now know that even the happy times can sometimes lead to a bit of struggle. Remember, we are humans hardwired for our comfort zone, but comfort zones don't allow for much change. Sometimes we need to look deep into our spiritual tool boxes and find those things that will help bring us back into a state of peace even in the best of times. Whether it's something unexpected or expected, change isn't easy. But by giving ourselves grace, we can navigate our way back.

In this book I share with you what I've learned over the years. I hope that you will find comfort in my words and find new tools to help you create the life that you deserve. I will discuss many specific topics throughout this book which helped me on my journey and my navigation back to peace again. I will also provide you some questions for self-reflection and journaling, if you so choose. My wish is that in my sharing you are able to find more of you, more of that beautiful soul here to live a magnificent life. Let's begin our journey together to help you feel more alive and passionate about the life you are living. Namaste, friends.

INTRODUCTION

Wisdom is the knowing that while you cannot control what is happening around you, it is always possible to change what is going on inside of you.

Who Are You?

The truth about who we are is that our souls come from a place of divine love. What's truly amazing about humans is that we have the capacity to change and adapt in every phase of our lives. Whatever life throws our way, we choose how it affects us. We are always given a choice although sometimes it may be hard to see this in the moment.

Isn't it interesting how whenever there is a baby around, everyone gathers around with a huge smile on their face? We start to use "baby talk" and cooing while completely falling in love with this little person in front of us. We become almost mesmerized at the sight of a newborn. There is no doubt that babies are adorable, but what is it that attracts the attention of humans with such intensity? There is an innocence to babies and even very young children that reminds us of where we came from and who we are at our core.

When we are born into this world, we live from our heart. Everything is new and exciting. We don't understand that there may be things which are unsafe around us. All we know is that we fully experience everything because we have nothing to compare to, meaning, no previous experiences would guide our actions. There are no caution signs in our head telling us to be scared or hold back. When older children or adults are around this energy, it draws them in with the remembrance of their true nature.

Fast forward to a time when, as adults, we've become so conditioned by society, family, parents, and school that we've forgotten where we came from. Remember the first time you got in trouble as a child? Or how about all the times you were told not to do something? Sadly, for us to function in our world, we are all required to learn rules. Rules about what is right or wrong, rules about how to act in social settings, rules about every aspect of functioning. For most of us, these rules eat away at our true nature over time and we forget who we are.

Most of us learned through many painful life experiences to shut down pieces of our heart. We became experts at "being strong," not showing our true emotions, and holding back what our heart wants to say in fear of the hurt that may come. On the other hand, we have all come across someone who shines light wherever they go. Their joy is palpable. These individuals smile often, speak positively about themselves and others, and share their hearts without reservation.

Remember the first time you felt a real attraction toward someone else, took a chance in sharing those feelings, and were rejected? Remember how horrible you felt? You may have said, "I'm never going to go through this again." What does this equate to? It equates to shutting down your heart, the most beautiful part of you.

None of us wants to be hurt. We don't want to feel pain, but in protecting our hearts to the point of walling them off, we don't allow ourselves to experience the magnificence of life. When we don't allow ourselves to feel the intensity of pain, we begin to lose the ability to feel the intensity of joy. We also lose our passion for life and forget who we are at a soul level when we shut down like this.

When asked the question of who we are, we may respond with statements such as, "I'm a doctor, a mom, a wife." These statements are all very true, but what about who you are *inside*. If we've shut down pieces of ourselves through conditioning, it makes it very hard to know our true nature. We can often go through many years, living day to day, not realizing something is missing until an event happens that turns our life upside down. For many of us, each struggle we experience moves us closer to the divine light of our soul. The universe has a way of helping us find our way back, and that way is by providing opportunities which help us awaken, if we so choose.

What is the purpose of awakening? Awakening by Merriam-Webster definition is "a coming into awareness." So, by experiencing an awakening, we are coming into an awareness of our true nature and purpose. We hear about those who have had near-death experiences and are able to articulate all the things they realized or found to be true afterward. Insights after these events are so extensive that some individuals have been able to heal themselves from illnesses which were on track to end their life. What this tells us is our souls have incredible abilities which we rarely tap into. If we can find a way to incorporate every part of our genuine self into our lives, imagine what we could create! And the exciting thing is, we are *all* capable of manifesting our dreams. The more we heal and find the parts of ourselves that we've hidden away, the greater our capacity to create.

Shortly after my divorce, my therapist asked me what I enjoyed doing outside of being a mom, wife, and nurse. Sadly, I had no idea because I had let those three roles define my life in such a way that I lost part of myself. I couldn't remember what it was that I enjoyed or who I was without those labels. I believe part of it was the grief I was experiencing, while part of it was the fact that I had given up pieces of myself while playing the necessary roles in my life. It took healing, time, and exploration for me to discover those parts of myself I'd forgotten as well as those parts I'd never explored in the past. In time I realized there was so much more to my existence than I had previously known. My world expanded in many ways once I was willing to open myself up and again allow new connections to form as well as explore new interests, all of which have led me to where I am today. In doing this, not only did I find the pieces I'd felt were missing but I also embraced my role as a mother and as a nurse with greater passion.

Reflection:

What events in your life may have led you to shutting down your true self and your heart?

What brings you the most joy and passion?

Who are you inside? If you're not sure, what actions might you take to help you find yourself?

_____
_____
_____
_____
_____
_____
_____
_____
_____
_____
_____
_____
_____
_____
_____
_____
_____
_____

JOURNEY TO PEACE AND HEALING

If I look through the clouds, I find a light which is my guide. That light is my soul always waiting for a clear day to shine.

Feeling Lost

There are times in our lives when we feel lost, unsure which direction to take. Very often, these feelings come as a result of grief we are moving through. We may have recently experienced some significant life changes or a loss which led to us feeling as if our life was turned upside down. Since we're creatures of habit, it's often very difficult to change our course unexpectedly when life throws us in different directions.

During my divorce, I remember waking up every morning feeling anxious, wishing things could go back to what I considered normal. I had a hard time facing my new reality because the loss was quite painful. I wasn't sure how to get through my days and often had to force myself to even get out of bed. I didn't think I could navigate my journey alone after being part of a unit and having a child together. I spent a great deal of time in tears trying to negotiate with some higher power to put things back as they had been previously. We all know that this was not possible and that I needed to find a way to move forward and create a new life.

There are many life events that happen which can lead to us feeling lost. As parents, an extremely painful time is when our children leave the nest. Our role for many years has been raising and protecting our young. Most of our energy goes into doing anything needed to fulfill this calling. For most parents, our children are our number one priority over careers and other relationships. When our children leave home, all of a sudden we experience a huge loss in purpose. I remember my son moving away to another state and the emptiness I felt inside. I had moved the year prior but only three hours away while he was finishing his last year of college. But when it was time for him to move away to another state, I felt lost. I wouldn't be able to easily visit whenever I wanted, he was starting his own life. I remember feeling that loss of purpose for weeks because he had always been the number one priority in my life.

These are only two examples of life situations in which one may feel lost, but there are many others, including loss of a parent, loss of a career, loss of health … The list is endless. I truly believe that if we can be gentle with ourselves while navigating this new and sometimes scary time of our lives we can come out on the other side feeling empowered. We must allow ourselves to feel the emotions coming up, sit with them, and give ourselves time to process. Having people we trust to share our experience with is extremely beneficial. There is always hope. A helpful first step is to acknowledge the grief we are feeling so we can work on healing it.

Reflection:

Journal about a time when you felt lost. What other emotions came up and how did you process them? Is there a specific action you took that helped you move forward?

_____
_____
_____
_____
_____
_____
_____
_____
_____
_____
_____
_____
_____
_____
_____
_____
_____
_____
_____
_____

Feeling lost usually points to a loss of something that matters to us, something our heart cherished.

The Grief Within

At the age of thirty, finding myself as a divorced single mom, I knew that something had to change in my life, and that change was *me*. I realized the saying "If nothing changes, nothing changes" held a great deal of validity. I didn't want to repeat some of my past mistakes, but I wasn't sure what or how to do things differently.

I initially took my sadness and poured it into helping others through my mission work. Flying to underdeveloped countries to provide medical care for children, many of whom had never seen a doctor, filled my heart. Every trip brought back my passion for life. Watching families through the experience of their children's congenital deformities being surgically repaired was a gift. I will never forget the look on a parent's face and the tears upon seeing their child for the first time after surgery. The tears of happiness as they knew their child could now be accepted instead of being ostracized. These children had huge hearts which filled up a room with love. The young ones weren't concerned with their cleft lip. In fact, they found happiness in the smallest of things. The families would sometimes walk for days to receive this needed medical care. They lived on very little and yet they were happy. There were no fancy houses, cars or clothes. These people were humble, kind, and extremely grateful. It always amazed me to see how happy they were despite having so little. When I was away for two weeks on these missions, I even found myself completely content without my comforts of home.

After a while, I found that putting my energy into my volunteer work didn't revive me as it once had. I ended up sick on a couple trips and although helping others was life-changing, something was still missing inside of me. I still often felt lost and alone, unsure of why I had this deep sense of sadness. I had a loving family, a great job, a beautiful home, and most importantly, an amazing son. Why couldn't I just be happy? Why did I feel like something was missing? I certainly filled my life with things and people I loved, but just couldn't figure out the missing piece.

The next decade of my life I chose to immerse myself in personal growth work. I went to seminars and workshops. I read books, watched movies, and connected with many individuals who followed a spiritual path that also attracted me. I became certified in Reiki, Past Life Regression. I wrote articles for an online magazine and participated as a writer in multiple published compilation books. In all of this there was a great deal of healing and finding myself again. There were times when I actually fooled myself into thinking I had no more healing to do. This all changed when I was forty-four.

While attending a personal growth seminar called Integrate, in which we learned the importance of integrating the parts of us we love with our shadow side, I met someone who would become an important part of my story. Shortly after Integrate, a family member shared a course she had gone through called the Grief Recovery Method, thinking we might be interested. Well, two months later I found myself going through this method, fully paid, by the man I'd met in Integrate. He wanted me to go through this certification course with him which at the time I found odd. My response was, "I don't have any grief." Despite my trying to get out of it, the universe had other ideas for me. So there I was, getting certified to be a Grief Recovery Specialist.

Grief to me was about the feelings one experiences due to the death of someone they love. Although I had experienced some death of family members, I felt that I'd dealt with it quite well. What I didn't realize until day one of certification training is that grief is actually a normal and natural response to a change or loss of any kind. *What?* This was something completely new to my ears. *You mean the loss I felt when I went through divorce was grief? The sadness I felt due to certain relationships in my life being less than I hoped for was grief? My difficulty with changing jobs when my hospital was on strike was grief?* I had no idea that the changes in familiar patterns of behavior could cause grief; I just knew I didn't feel good inside. A part of me felt empty and lost. But I figured with time, I would feel better and life would move on. Besides, I'd done a good job of distracting myself from grief for most of my adult life.

Over the course of four days, I realized (like most people) I'd been carrying around a large amount of grief for years. I'd finally identified the missing puzzle piece to my emptiness that I often experienced. I learned that grief is cumulative and always negatively cumulative. The longer we live, the more our backpack fills up, especially if we don't take actions to heal what's hurting us. I learned that past grief was affecting every aspect of my life at the present moment and keeping me from being fully present. And I learned that time alone doesn't heal anything. We must take actions within time in order to heal our broken heart just as we must take actions within time to heal a broken leg.

Unfortunately, most of us are not taught what to do when our heart hurts. We are taught basic first aid as we are growing up. We know what to do if we fall down and skin our knee, but we often don't know what to do if our heart is bleeding emotionally. Grief isn't a concept most families discuss when growing up. If parents aren't taught that grief is a normal and natural reaction to loss or change, they won't be able to pass this insight on to their children. We often hear things such as, "You will be ok. You will find someone new. They are in a better place. Be strong. Keep busy. You will feel better in time." Yikes!! While people mean well with these statements, they do not honor the feelings of the person who is grieving. And most of the time, these types of unhelpful statements end the sharing which is coming from the griever.

Most of us learn well the "Academy Award Winning Behaviors" as talked about in the Grief Recovery Method. These are behaviors we engage in to make others think we are doing just fine. "Be strong" is a behavior that often starts in childhood. We grew up in families in which we had to figure out a way to get through the days despite uncomfortable things in our family unit. Be strong and push through. Unfortunately, this often leads to the closing of our hearts and pushing people away—exactly the opposite of which we really want—but we work hard to protect our hearts.

Along with being strong, we may isolate. By bottling up our feelings and not sharing, we end up becoming loners by choice. We don't want anyone to know we are hurting. The best way to keep this away from others is to stay away from everyone.

On another extreme, we will "replace the loss." My dog died, so let's go get a new puppy. My husband left me, so I'll find a new man in my life. Replacing a loss may trick you into thinking you've healed. You may feel better momentarily. That is, until the newness wears off and you realize that using something to replace something you're grieving absolutely does not help your healing. In fact, you then end up with more grief from the extra things you've added to your life without healing the previous.

Grief is like our shadow. If we don't heal, it follows us around for life. We often engage in STERB's (short-term, energy-relieving behaviors) to help us feel good. The funny thing about grief is that it keeps rearing its ugly head, knocking at our door and causing problems until we take a good hard look at it.

In the meantime, humans engage in many activities to "not feel or distract themselves from feeling." Why do you think people become addicts? Because some part of them is hurting inside. Using alcohol, drugs, nicotine, gaming, gambling, excessive shopping or eating, among others helps us "feel" better. These STERB's give us the illusion of healing but require we engage in them more frequently as the illusion wears off after a short period of time.

We can't run from our internal grief forever, and it just keeps accumulating over time. Our backpack gets so full that we have a hard time handling the weight of it. Perhaps you have felt overwhelmed, stuck, or that life is so heavy you simply don't have the energy to do anything? We do have a choice, though, and that is to actually learn how to heal our heart and process the grief that has accumulated over our lifetime. Apparently, this is what the universe had in mind for me as I sat in the seminar room for four days learning about the Grief Recovery Method.

During the days of my seminar with the Grief Recovery Institute, and for many months after, I questioned the actions of the method. Was my heart really healing from the hurt? Did I feel more alive inside? The answer didn't come right away because the work doesn't just happen in four days. Our grief is like an artichoke. There are many layers caused by multiple events over our lifetime. At the center is our heart, which we've built big walls around to protect it from pain. Each leaf of the artichoke is another hurt, and as we peel back each of the leaves, we get to the heart. The heart is the part in need of healing. While that may sound absolutely overwhelming, it's actually exciting because realizing there are layers means we can take a look at what has been weighing us down and then CHOOSE to do something with our feelings.

Most of us look back on events and realize we have regrets about what we could have done or said differently. The Grief Recovery Method taught me how important it is to stay current in our relationships. By staying current, we are less likely to experience the feelings of regret. I know there were so many things I wish I had said and done prior to my Dad passing away. After he was gone, I had deep regrets for a long time. It was the Grief Recovery Method that helped me heal the pain inside my heart and be able to think of that relationship after he was gone without the burden of the deep pain. I could again feel complete with our relationship and hold the love in my heart next to the good memories, instead of the pain.

Many of us have also experienced events or transgressions against us that we have difficulty forgiving. I know it's extremely difficult to forgive when we have been the victim of an event that led to deep pain. And I remind myself that forgiveness isn't for another person, it's for us. It doesn't mean the event didn't happen or was in any way okay; it means we choose to move on and allow ourselves to heal. Forgiveness doesn't ever excuse another individual's hurtful behavior, which is important to remember. It allows us to experience joy again without the constant pain. It allows us to move forward instead of staying stuck in the past which hurt us.

I remember after my divorce the pain I felt knowing my husband had given up on our marriage. He had chosen to leave, thus no longer working to keep our family together. I experienced a great deal of anger during this time and absolute disbelief that he was to the point of not wanting to even work on repairing our relationship. I didn't want to forgive and certainly I wasn't going to forget. I carried around resentment for years and made my choice to let this affect my life. Sadly, it took me a bit before I took a good hard look at what had happened and started taking ownership for my part in our failed marriage. It was easier, at first, to blame him than it was to look deep inside and feel the pain from knowing my contribution.

The beauty of healing our hearts is also getting to a place of forgiveness. As I mentioned previously, forgiveness doesn't mean the transgression never happened or even make it acceptable, it allows us to move on and no longer hold resentment and pain in our hearts. We deserve to have a heart which is full of light and love versus darkness, but in order to experience this, we must let go of those things which bring us pain.

By working through my own grief, I am able to not only extend forgiveness to those around me but also to myself, which is sometimes even more difficult. I remember years after my divorce, once I'd worked through the grief behind the loss of our family unit, feeling an extreme amount of gratitude for my ex-husband. I could see the gifts that he'd given me on my journey. I could see my part in the dissolution of our marriage. I was able to move forward in a healthy way for both of us and our son. And I was able to verbalize my gratitude for him and my apologies for ways in which I'd hurt our marriage and him as an individual.

Now, this ending doesn't happen for every relationship which we've healed. However, this is possible, and when it's obtained it brings about a great sense of peace to our hearts and our minds. Letting go of that which we've held onto with a death grip lifts a very substantial weight off of us and allows new light into our lives. While forgiveness is ultimately for us personally, it can at times provide a new sense of peace for others involved as well.

Reflection:

What grief do you carry that affects the quality of your life?

Are there times you wish a certain relationship was more, had been better, or different?

Who or what situation have you not offered forgiveness to in your heart and mind? What has held you back from forgiving?

_____
_____
_____
_____
_____
_____
_____
_____
_____
_____
_____
_____
_____

JOURNEY TO PEACE AND HEALING

The grief that we hold inside is that which controls our life. To be free we must choose to look at our unresolved grief and take action to heal it.

Feel, Heal, Reveal

One thing I learned through my own personal struggle is that for me to become the best possible version of myself, it's imperative that I first heal the parts of me that hurt. There were many times that I wanted to ignore my pain inside, push it down, and move on. I didn't have time, or so I thought, to deal with what I considered "negative" energy inside. It felt easier to ignore all of this and work on figuring out who I am or what gifts I bring to this world that I could share with others. I was surprised to discover it doesn't work in that order.

Prior to experiencing the greatest gifts in life, we must first *heal*. And in order to heal, we must feel. That feeling word again that makes so many uncomfortable. Yes, it's necessary to feel in order to heal. We must allow ourselves to process the emotions that come up for us surrounding events of our past. Like we discussed earlier, most of us find ways to push down those emotions and bury them. We use alcohol, drugs, electronics, shopping, and other distractions to keep us from feeling. Until we stop covering up our emotions we can't possibly begin to heal and reveal our true soul's purpose.

Wanting to shine as a bright light and make a difference in the world, I tried to push through the grief from past experiences. I thought that by helping others, my wounds would be healed. What I found was that although helping others greatly benefited my life and started my journey to healing, it in no way provided the healing I needed. There was work to be done on my part and things I had to take a good hard look at in order to move forward in a healthy way.

After my divorce, I was struggling to keep my house, juggle all the responsibilities of a single mom, and work. As much as I was hurting, I also didn't feel I had the time to focus on my own pain, and frankly, it felt quite dismal to do so. Unfortunately, I found that every little thing that happened which stretched me, hurt, or was uncomfortable led to a reaction that seemed more extreme than necessary. I'd find myself angry, crying, lashing out, and unable to deal with situations in a healthy way. My grief was accumulating because I was trying to ignore it and move forward. However, ignoring the pain inside never works—at least not for very long. It eventually rears its ugly head and lets you know it's still there.

It's not easy or even fun to dig deep and find our shadows that keep cropping up. But when we try to ignore them, we find that they are peeking around every corner we turn. They want to be noticed, recognized, and loved into healing. It's not a punishment but actually a gift to process our grief and move forward in healthier ways. Not only does our pain help others through our healing but it also allows our light to shine even brighter than we imagined. We learn that to empower others, we first must empower ourselves. Going within leads to the places we've dreamed about for our lives. It brings us peace.

If you're like me, you want to feel better *now*, move forward, and focus on something different. I'm finally able to be graceful and patient as I navigate difficult emotions. I understand that by allowing whatever I'm feeling to be "okay," it's easier to work through anything that comes up. I know that while things may not exactly work on my timeline, they work on the universe's timeline, which makes it perfect.

Our lives are perfectly devised for our own learning and growth. We all made choices before incarnating to have particular experiences on this earth to help our own evolution. If you are reading this book, I'm betting you've experienced a great deal of growth during your time here and know that your presence has a significant purpose. You also know your purpose starts with your own self-care and healing.

It is often in our own healing that we discover our purpose and how we can guide others on their journey. If we look at our world as a collective of souls here to help one another, we understand that each one of us possess gifts that we can share with others. This reminds me of long ago when life was navigated through trade. You might have paid for your doctor's visit with a chicken or traded one type of vegetable or meat with a farmer for something they raised. In some ways, these sound like simpler times, and what a beautiful exchange of energy. By focusing on our own healing and allowing it to reveal our innate gifts, we can choose to use this as an energy exchange with others. This is how we support one another on our path.

Please don't interpret this as you needing to have some expensive degree or big talent. The most beautiful exchange of energy is often one of love. A simple gesture of love expressed or shown to another can actually change a life. For someone to know they are unconditionally cared for when they may not have experienced this prior to this moment is a BIG thing. So many feel alone, and knowing that others can relate or that they care really does go a long way. Your healed heart can shine more love and light into the world than you could have ever thought possible. And with this love and light, you empower others to do the same.

Reflection:

In the past, after you've allowed yourself to heal from something painful, do you ever remember feeling propelled forward into your purpose? Journal about this and what you learned during this time.

Do you feel stuck right now in life? If so, what areas would you like to focus on healing?

What are you willing to let go of to be able to move forward in your own life?

_____
_____
_____
_____
_____
_____
_____
_____
_____
_____
_____
_____
_____
_____
_____

FEEL, HEAL, REVEAL

Until we feel, we are unable to heal. Until we heal, we keep our greatest gifts hidden from the world.

Fear

What thoughts come to mind when you hear the word "fear"? Does it create a sense of anxiety? Do you feel a restriction in your chest or breathing? Fear manifests differently for everyone. Visions may come to mind that represent experiences from our own lives that caused us to feel scared. Unfortunately, we often associate fear with something negative, being in harm's way, or getting hurt. Fear can also be an emotion which helps show us where we need to focus or areas in which we could grow.

Feeling afraid doesn't always equate to a harmful experience in our lives. Sometimes we are afraid to let go or move forward. We may feel afraid to start something new or end something that no longer serves a purpose in our soul growth. Sometimes it's difficult to tell the difference between fear coming up due to potential harm or that which is normal because we are doing something new, making a change. Sometimes it's a combination of both that gives us these emotions that stir us up inside.

Recently, I went on my first backpacking trip with my son. At the end of our first day, we had to hike up through brush and over large boulders to make it to camp. My pack was heavy, my legs were fatigued, and I was literally scared I would fall while attempting the final leg of this hike. This feeling was coming not only from my concerns surrounding a potential fall and injury but also the unknown since, even though I was an experienced hiker, this was my first time hiking with 25 pounds on my back.

Thankfully, my son helped with my pack and I was able to push through the last grueling part to make it to camp. As I sat at camp that night, I began to worry about how I would get back down the mountain and what the rest of our trip would look like.

I found myself feeling frustrated that my confidence was lacking in this new experience. I had been hiking for years, so why was this trip with my son any different? What was I afraid of in this moment? Being successful on this adventure was important to me and I was afraid of failure. After all, the first day I managed to fall and skin up both of my knees in the first couple hours. With these feelings inside, how was I going to push forward and make this a growing experience?

The second night I knew that it was important for me to change my mindset from one of fear to one of empowerment. I knew I could do this and be successful. I rarely fail at things in my life. I reminded myself of my track record with success as I envisioned our hike through the beautiful mountains. I reminded myself that my fear was normal as I was venturing into a new territory with this backpacking journey. And lastly, I assured myself I was safe and free from any harm.

I'm a believer in angels, guides, and those who have passed being ever present, providing support and protection when asked, so I invoked their help on my journey as well. The next day we got up, packed up camp, and with my new empowered thoughts, we made it safely back to the car without any falls or mishaps. It was another great example of how changing our thoughts can greatly change our experience.

Personally, I know how easy it is to stay stuck in familiar patterns. Fear of change may bring about feelings of sadness, loss, failure, and many other emotions we view as less than joyful. Often it takes us a great deal to get to the point in which we are willing to make a change. The universe can keep throwing opportunities and signs our way, but we may ignore them because our comfort zone is familiar, whereas change creates unknowns. We end up burned out, sick, and depleted before we choose to jump out of what no longer serves us and try something new. I've been there and done that so many times in my life, and it's not a comfortable place to be. I try to remind myself that on the other side of fear is opportunity and open doors. After the initial leap of faith, there is usually a sense of calm and peace I feel inside, letting me know that the universe is supporting me, I will be fine and I've stepped back onto a path which is more beneficial to my overall well-being.

One may wonder how we get a sense of knowing or "feel" calm and peaceful with large life changes. It's taken years for me to develop and trust my own intuition and inner sense, which guides my life. Again, I spent many times scared of trusting what I felt but over time I realized that without feelings of anxiety inside, I can trust my inner knowing. There are definitely times when my mind thinks about a decision I'm making and wants to get the ego involved. I hear, "Are you crazy? What are you thinking? What about ____?" I've come to realize if I listen to my ego and acknowledge its fears, it will then quiet so I can hear my soul speaking, my intuition.

About twenty years ago I opened a fortune cookie which said, "You need not worry about your future." This has been in my wallet since that time and is a constant reminder that no matter what I encounter on my journey I will be fine. It's funny because most of the time I forget about this little slip of paper in my wallet. But when fear creeps in related to trying something new or a life change I hear the words in my head again, "You need not worry about your future." I've come to trust in this knowing that all will be well and work out. We cannot always see that in the middle of a crisis or uncomfortable situation. Trusting that the universe has our well-being in mind allows us to move through situations knowing that what comes next will be in our best interest and for our overall growth.

Reflection:

In what areas do you let fear hold you back?

Think of one situation currently in your life which leads to fear-centered emotions. Where is your fear coming from? If you know there is a change you are being called to make, what is one first step you can take? Reflect on these questions.

_____
_____
_____
_____
_____
_____
_____
_____
_____
_____
_____
_____
_____
_____
_____

Fear often makes us believe that we are in danger when, really, we are about ready to leap into something new and foreign to us. Trust in the knowing that all will be well whatever detours life chooses to take.

The Power of The Mind

Ever notice that your life often reflects your own thoughts? Our minds are very powerful; in fact, they are so powerful they have the ability to create the life of our dreams through our thoughts and feelings. We are magnificent manifesting creatures!

Remember back to a day when you woke up in the morning just dreading going to work. Your thoughts were pessimistic and you may have felt frustrated and angry inside. Usually, when we start this way, our day ends up being filled with one mishap, frustration, and argument after another. By the end of the day, we want to hide in a hole and not come out until the world changes.

In contrast, think back to a day you woke up with positive thoughts and told yourself it's going to be a good day. Things may have occurred that led to frustration, but you likely reacted with patience and let things slide. When you focused on the good, you were rewarded with more good drawn to you.

It's easy to not take notice of how we can experience two completely different days. Changing our focus doesn't fix everything, but what it does do is change our perspective. We attract the same energy we put out into the universe. So put out positive thoughts and I bet you will see more positive than negative. The trick is your feelings must match your thoughts. Think about something that brings you joy and hold that in your awareness. As much as possible, allow that to be the primary feeling throughout the day. See if it makes a difference in the kind of day you have.

A Simple Story About Thoughts Become Things and the Law of Attraction

If you have any hesitation believing that your thoughts are powerful and you attract what's happening inside of you, it's fun to once in a while test the theory. The most important thing to realize is that if you're "trying" to believe that something will manifest, but your feelings don't truly match what you are thinking about, you will not see results. We must match our thoughts, beliefs, and feelings in order to manifest. This is definitely not an easy task. It takes practice as well as learning when you are truly in the right mindset versus desperate for something to change in your life.

For example, my son and I were vacationing at a beach in Northern California where we agreed to meet for a few days. On one of the days when we were just hanging out at the house, I decided to go down to the beach while he was doing some work on his computer. I told my son as I was heading out to walk on the beach that I was determined to find a sand dollar. He told me that it was too late in the day and I likely wouldn't come across any sand dollars. The important thing to know is this area has a very rocky coastline. The only thing I saw every time I went down to the beach were rocks and broken shells, but not even one broken sand dollar. He was skeptical I would come back with a sand dollar, but I was convinced. I pictured it in my mind and I felt the joy behind finding one, holding it in my hand.

When I didn't find any sand dollars at the first beach, I shrugged my shoulders and said to myself, "I will find one at the next beach." A short drive down the road, I stopped and began walking. First, I only found small broken pieces of shells and parts of sand dollars. Then all of a sudden, I came across a whole, perfect sand dollar! My excitement increased as I held it in my hand with the knowing that my beliefs helped me find what I was looking for at the beach.

This wasn't the first time I'd successfully manifested a sand dollar on an otherwise barren beach. Years back, my significant other was feeling a bit down in the dumps. I was explaining that our thoughts can become things and we are very powerful at manifesting both what we want and what we don't want. We also happened to be at the beach, this time in Oregon, and I asked him to manifest finding a sand dollar. He really wasn't interested in playing this game so I took it upon myself to believe and feel into finding this special sand dollar. He, like my son, was skeptical, but I was persistent in my "knowing" that this was going to happen. As we walked and the minutes passed, whenever my beliefs wavered, I reminded myself that my mind is powerful. I felt into my desire and again pictured its manifestation. Sure enough, a short time later, not only did I find one perfect sand dollar but I found two!

It's easier to create things in our life when we are feeling full of light, love, and passion. It's when we are struggling in darker times that we forget our abilities. In these times it's more difficult to hold positive thoughts, feelings, and beliefs. Instead, we often find ourselves in dark places, perhaps feeling sad, hopeless, depresssed. The world around us then mirrors these thoughts. It takes most people a lot of effort to get out of this space. Sometimes we need an event to "wake us up" again but the hope is that the event isn't one that's extremely painful to us. I personally have my "tribe" of friends and family whom I reach out to when I find myself in this space. They remind me of who I am and what I'm capable of. These are my people who cheer me on and believe in me without doubt. They help me find my center again and provide support for me to continue creating that which I desire in my life.

The question for each of us is what are we creating? Are we creating the peaceful life we desire? This is definitely not an easy task when life around us is full of chaos and turbulence. We live in a time where electronics have all but taken over our world. We are inundated every day with computers at work, smart phones at home. TV, news, social media feeding us information that for the most part does not foster a feeling of peace within our minds. Tragedy from natural disasters, violence and war weigh heavy on our hearts. This doesn't even include tragedy in our own lives or those of people we love. Our hearts can only handle so much of this pain until they start to shut down and stop "feeling."

How does this hardening of our heart affect our lives? When we block our hearts from feeling joy, love, light and passion we are unable to manifest these things. The Law of Attraction states we attract more of our own energy. That's a hard one to digest when we are struggling in our own pain and grief. We certainly don't want any more of what we are currently experiencing, but how do we get ourselves into a place where we can attract the things we desire. We know we have to change our own energy and we also know at certain moments all we can do is make it through the day.

At the most difficult times of my life, I've told myself if a day seems like a long time, how about focusing on getting through the next hour or the next minute. Breaking things down into smaller time periods can make the rough moments more tolerable. We can feel proud of ourselves for getting by moment to moment. Nothing lasts forever, but sometimes it feels like the pain won't end. And when we feel stuck, it may feel like things will never change. We want something different, but it's not going to happen overnight.

When I got divorced, I felt miserable. My pain was overwhelming—to the point of me wanting to just stay in bed all day long. But this wasn't possible being a mom and a nurse with a job. I didn't know how things would change. I wanted a magical wand to make things better.

It was the little things I started to do which shifted my energy (like my mission trips) enough to give my life a different trajectory. Mission trips are actually more than something little I did but at the time changing my focus was what helped me the most. This allowed me to start finding ways to heal my heart. In the twenty years since my divorce, I've learned many other tools to shift my energy in a positive way which we will focus on in coming chapters. For now, I leave you with a few questions to ponder and perhaps journal about.

Reflection:

What energy do you believe you are putting out into the world most of the time?

What are you attracting into your life with the energy you put out into the world?

Are there any changes you would like to make in order to manifest differently?

Exercise:

Think of something small, either a change or an object, you want to manifest in your life. It needs to be something you can feel into and believe you can manifest. Start small. Perhaps brainstorm, then sit quietly and meditate about it. Make sure your heart can feel the joy in this manifestation. Journal about this journey of manifestation. And most importantly, whatever happens, be graceful with yourself. It takes practice to manifest our dreams.

_____
_____
_____
_____
_____
_____
_____
_____

THE POWER OF THE MIND

I am a capable, powerful being able to manifest my dreams and desires. I believe in my ability and use my mind and heart to create that which brings me more joy, passion, and love.

Releasing

There are times throughout our life when we want to continue to hold onto things that are no longer serving us. Whether it's a job, a relationship, a home, or a belief, it may feel extremely difficult to change something in our life when it's become our "normal" and "comfort zone." But by holding on, we don't allow our spirit to roam free. For a multitude of reasons, we keep ourselves in our own "prison," trying to endure what's not working.

I don't know about you, but I've always been one of those people who is super responsible. For me, this meant taking care of everyone else, following rules, going to college, getting the good job with benefits, buying the home. I can go on and on. Some of this greatly benefited me but I also restricted myself through my belief system. I've believed there was a way I needed to do things and structure my life. While this belief led me on a wonderful journey which helped me grow, it also kept me from growing in many other ways.

Growing up around alcoholism, I developed a coping mechanism which involved keeping everything very much intact, in line, together. My belief was that by being "good," doing what was expected of me, following the rules, and keeping my thoughts to myself, it would lead to a more peaceful household. I believed that somehow my behavior would make things better.

It took years for me to learn that when someone we love is an addict, we cannot change their behavior or make things better for them. I can now see that my lack of speaking up was, in a way, enabling the behavior. It definitely did not honor my own life.

Sadly, chaos became normal for me. For many years into my young adulthood, I surrounded myself in more chaos, often creating it. Calm felt uncomfortable and foreign to me, something I didn't know how to navigate. I was always waiting for the other shoe to drop. It took courage to heal my heart and the deep hurt inside. This healing ultimately led me to a life in which chaos is no longer normal, and calm is what I choose to surround myself with.

Since my childhood, I have struggled with change and often chose to keep things in my life which did not serve my highest good. And while some of my relationships were extremely painful, as I endured ongoing chaos in them, I also don't regret my path since it led me to where I am today. Had I "let go" sooner, my path would have looked different. Although one will never know what may have been.

What I know today is that in learning to let go and release things which no longer serve me, I allow myself to take the next step on my journey of growth. The letting-go process may feel extremely uncomfortable in the planning and implementing. I also know that once one takes action to release, there is often a sense of freedom. I compare it to being able to take a deep breath after holding one's breath for quite some time. One usually realizes how hard they had been trying to hold on to something that no longer provided joy, peace, and harmony.

Although parts of letting go may be painful, it also allows the universe to bring other things in to fill the void that may be left. Opportunities show up. Doors begin to open where previously

RELEASING

there had been locks in which one could not access the other side. The perfect people show up at the perfect time, the ones you need to help you on the next part of your journey. Your job is to believe. Believe in yourself. Believe in the support of the universe.

Reflection:

What beliefs are you holding that no longer serve you?

How are these beliefs keeping you from letting go of things in your life?

What would you like to release moving forward?

How might your life change by releasing these things?

What are you not allowing by holding on so tight?

_____
_____
_____
_____
_____
_____
_____
_____
_____
_____
_____
_____
_____
_____
_____

RELEASING

It is the power of letting go that allows the universe to open new doors.

Transition

*I*f you can raise your hand and honestly tell me you love change, I commend you. Most of us feel a sense of dread with big life changes even if there is a part that excites us. I remember when I sold my home of 24 years, in which I raised my son, and moved almost four hours away. Even though part of my family lived where I was moving, my son had already moved out of the house, and I was going to live somewhere I'd always wanted to reside, it felt uncomfortable.

The first month I remember my kitty meowing at all hours of the night and jumping up onto the bed, keeping us awake after the move. She wasn't familiar with her new home. The surroundings which had always provided comfort were no longer around. I had to adapt to not having my own space and sharing a home with someone new. I was used to all of my belongings and a house being organized the way I preferred. Now most of my belongings were in a storage unit and I was living in a home furnished by my significant other. With patience and a great deal of love, we both adapted to our new home, but the transition was not an easy one for any of us.

Just like our animals, we need to allow ourselves space and time when going through life transitions. To expect that it's going to be easy and without a little bit of discomfort is setting ourselves up for hard times. We may be very excited about our new life, but leaving the old one is leaving our comfort zone (even if it wasn't comfortable). Allowing ourselves to go through a multitude of emotions and being okay with whatever they are is one of the secrets to moving forward with greater ease. Giving yourself extra love and calling in your tribe of people who can rally around on the tough days can make the transition less difficult and provide the support to carry you through. It can take us by surprise when we find that sometimes even changes which are for the best create a great deal of anxiety.

Shortly after my divorce, I discovered ways to get through anxiety-producing events and experiences. Anyone who has ever experienced significant anxiety knows how crippling it can be. It's impossible to make decisions or function normally. Anxiety makes everything feel like walking through quicksand. You are trying to stay above the sand but feel yourself sinking deeper and deeper. It's a very uneasy feeling that you never forget. By focusing on just one moment at a time, I found it bearable. No need to focus on the entire day or the future as that would lead to more anxiety. Focusing on getting through the next hour or sometimes even the next minute allows your mind to relax just a little bit more.

Often we take our current feeling or experience and think that it will never feel better. We don't know how things will improve and can't see our way from the dark back into the light. By breaking up our thinking into very small increments of time, it keeps us in the present moment instead of projecting into the future. It keeps our mind from going to some very dismal places which usually gets us out of the dark faster.

If you believe thoughts become things, then focusing on how painful the future will be often brings about more pain. In contrast, staying in the moment and allowing hope for the hours and days ahead, you attract good back into your life.

This is not to say that all transitions are anxiety-producing, but sometimes just the unknown of what may be in the future can cause distress. As I write this book, I've currently decided to leave my nursing job, uncertain about my path for the future. While this transition is one I'm very much excited about, if I spend too much time in my head about the "what if's," anxiety creeps into my thoughts. Trusting in our transitions and our future can help provide peace during these times.

Reflection:

During periods of transition, how do you normally feel? Do you tend to think about the "what if's" or trust in the universe?

How can you be more gentle with yourself during transition?

What types of self-care can you practice during transitional times?

_____
_____
_____
_____
_____
_____
_____
_____
_____
_____
_____
_____
_____
_____
_____

TRANSITION

If you trusted in the universe to always support you, what changes would you make in your own life?

The Power of "No"

From an early age, most of us heard the word "no" multiple times a day. When we were young, our parents used no to protect us. As we'd start to touch a hot stove or run out in traffic, the first thing we would hear is a loud "NO." Then, as we become older, the word has many other meanings for us. Maybe we apply for a new job and we are told that we didn't get it or ask someone out on a date and get rejected. "NO" begins to have a very negative energy behind it by the time we are adults functioning in society.

Fast forward to a time when we are struggling to keep up in our lives. Marriage, kids, house, job, pets, extracurricular activities. Pretty soon we barely have time to breathe with everything we've fit into our lives. And then someone comes up to us and says, "Why don't you say no?" *Wait, what?* Our entire life we've grown to very much dislike the word no and our bodies seem to have a negative reaction to hearing it. So, why would we say no to something? Ah, perhaps it's time to retrain our minds about what saying no can actually mean.

Remember back to being a toddler and your mom or dad told you no? Again, that was to protect you. It wasn't meant as a punishment. It was said because at that age, we aren't capable of knowing how to take care of ourselves. Our parents fill the role that is turned over to us when we become older. But now, as adults, we find it so hard to say no, set boundaries, and protect ourselves. We may have come to believe that by saying "no," we are doing something bad. In reality, when we choose to set boundaries, we are actually focusing on self-care.

Self-care is such a foreign concept to those of us who have grown up in families where we either took care of our siblings or our parents for much of our younger years. Some of us were taught that if you aren't focusing on what you can do for others, you are being selfish. This belief leads us to "burning the candle on both ends." Unfortunately, over time, this constant giving leads to burn out, illness, and depression, among other things. Far too many end up divorced, sick, in abusive relationships, hating their jobs, or worse.

What took me a long time to figure out is that without giving to myself first, I have nothing to give to others. My empty tank has literally no fuel, so it keeps trying to scrape from the bottom, but there is nothing there. I end up even more burned out, resentful, and depressed in the knowing that my ability to give is depleted. And this is where boundaries come into play.

We hear about boundaries quite often and sometimes find it hard to understand how important they are for our lives. It's not hard to see that we must set boundaries to keep our relationships healthy or other areas of our life, but boundaries don't always have to be big "no's." Boundaries can also be small ways in which we care for ourselves. Saying no is a way in which we set boundaries.

There have been times in my life in which I've run around trying to be a life preserver to anyone and everyone suffering. While it seems like a very selfless thing to do it's impossible to hold everyone afloat as well as staying above the water yourself. The more people we have holding on to us, the greater the likelihood we will go under. This isn't to say we shouldn't reach out and be there for others. It's just important that we set our own boundaries.

What does this look like?

First, it's important that before we reach out to lift others up, we must fill our own vessel. Are you tired, overwhelmed, stressed? Or are you well rested, settled, peaceful? These are two completely different energy levels. If we are feeling depleted, we must make the time to find a way to fill ourselves back up. Sometimes this is sleep, quiet time, meditation, a walk in the outdoors. Other times we need to shut off our phone or get away for a few days to just be alone. There is no right answer. If we don't focus on our needs, we end up further depleted which can actually be detrimental to those around us that we may be trying to support as well.

Conversely, if we can step away from things in our life for a bit of time, we can focus on self-care. I've heard many say over the years that they feel taking time for themselves is "selfish" or they just don't have time because there are too many other things to tend to. I understand both of these arguments. None of us want to feel selfish or make life all about us. However, if we don't put ourselves first, at least sometimes, we are not able to function at a level that allows us to show up authentically for others. Yes, there will always be many things to take care of. It's never ending. Work, children, laundry, yard work, errands, bills, family to name a few. And these will be ever present in our lives. By not stepping away and making time to fill ourselves back up, we are unable to provide for others or be the bright shining light in the world that we want to be.

The more we ignore our own needs and keep pushing through, the greater the chance our bodies will start sending some red flags.

Our physical health and our mental health suffer when we forget to care for ourselves. This is usually after our relationships and job have already suffered. I can't count the number of times when I started suffering from one ailment or another. I'd have symptoms that no doctor could explain and my frustration would be mounting as the tests revealed normal results. It usually came down to me taking a long hard look at what was going on in my life.

- Was there something incredibly stressful that I was dealing with at the time?

- Were there things that weighed heavily on my mind or my heart?

- Did I have some relationships that were not healthy for me to be engaged in anymore?

After my Dad passed away, I began having chest discomfort, shortness of breath, and heart palpitations. Multiple medical tests showed I was just fine physically. What was wrong was grief filling my heart from the loss, leading to physical symptoms. These symptoms kept resurfacing until I was able to find a way to process my feelings. Of course, processing grief means we must take actions within time. It's important to find ways in which we can support our body, mind, and heart while working on our own healing. We will talk about tools to help move through these times in pages ahead but let's keep our focus right now on self-care.

It's just not always easy to make that time for self-care. To this I say, "Can you make 10 minutes in a day for you?" Ten minutes doesn't seem like very long when in fact there are 1,440 minutes in a day. If we assume most of us are sleeping around 8 hours a day that still leaves 960 minutes a day in which we are awake. And isn't it interesting that sometimes we feel taking 10 minutes for self-care is impossible to fit into our day? I'm as guilty as anyone else in saying, "I don't have time." Well, what about the minutes I've wasted looking at social media, email, news stories? Couldn't I have used that time to do something for myself? Sometimes you really just have to force self-care. If you find being at home a distraction, go sit in a park while leaving your phone in the car or at home. Find a forest or a body of water to spend time in. Sit on a rock by a river/creek. Ignore the outside world for a short time. Breathe and let the air fill your lungs up with energy. Our bodies deserve this much attention and more.

The more we make time for self-care, the more we realize its importance. We begin to feel rejuvenated, lighter, and full of life. Our energy begins to shift. We have more to share with others. Our hearts feel open again. We find that taking 10 minutes for ourselves turns into 30 turns into 60 and maybe more. People around us begin to see a change and ask about it as they are attracted to our brighter light. Saying no to others and yes to ourselves can lead to our life changing in magical ways, allowing us to create from a place of fullness versus a place of lack.

Reflection:

In what areas of your life would you like to say "no" more often?

What does self-care mean to you?

In what ways do you make time for yourself?

Are there ways in which you would like to implement more self-care?

_____
_____
_____
_____
_____
_____
_____
_____
_____
_____
_____
_____
_____
_____

THE POWER OF "NO"

When I say no to others, I say yes to myself. In saying yes to myself, my ability to show up for others in the future increases exponentially. Self-care creates a richer life for me and for those whose lives I touch.

Boundaries

When considering boundaries, we may think about how we choose to set them in relationships or where our boundaries may need some adjusting. Sometimes we are afraid to set boundaries for the fear of people we love walking out of our lives. For those of us who didn't always have two parental figures consistently in our lives throughout our childhood, the last thing we want is one more person abandoning us. Due to this fear, we may tolerate behaviors from others that are less than loving and that don't honor our worth. Saying no, setting boundaries, and letting others know what we will and will not accept takes bravery and courage. Knowing that we are worth it and deserve only the best is imperative to us having what we deserve.

Just as we must set boundaries in our relationships, it's also necessary to set them in other areas of our lives such as jobs/careers. Many of us feel that we must accept whatever we encounter at work even if it feels harmful to our own well-being. Our ingrained belief that our responsibility is to continue working in our job to provide for ourselves and our family despite the treatment we receive or unhealthy patterns we encounter is often to our detriment. This belief keeps us in jobs way past the time we should be in them and often leads us to health issues due to the stress we carry around daily. When we spend more time at work than we do outside of it, our life begins to reflect our feelings around our work. If we are unhappy and stressed, it's very difficult to step outside of work feeling joyful, calm, and peaceful. This lack of passion leads to other areas of our life suffering.

So why do we find it so hard to leave a job? From childhood we are often taught that being responsible means carrying a full-time job with benefits. We watched our parents working tirelessly, many times multiple jobs. What we grew up with, we repeat in our own lives. The problem is that in the current era, our world is not as simple as it was previously. We are constantly inundated with things we need to do, places we need to go, and busyness. We may have a hard time even finding moments to spend with our extended family, friends, or practice self-care. This quickly leads to burnout and exhaustion.

Feeling exhausted due to work sometimes isn't even enough to make us walk away and decide to do something different. We have conflicting feelings and thoughts. We may want to leave, but we also work with many people whom we call our friends. We may feel guilty about leaving others when the situations aren't good at work, knowing they will be left with an even heavier workload. It's hard to put ourselves first and understand that we must put our own oxygen mask on before helping others. Unfortunately, as the plane is going down, we can't save others if we don't first focus on us. This is not easy when you are someone who has historically put others first. You don't want to let people down, so you keep trying to help others around you while you yourself are quickly sinking.

Interestingly enough, as I'm writing this book, I've struggled with my own personal boundaries, feeling stuck in a job which no longer benefits my life except financially. I've advocated for changes for quite some time to no avail. I've watched many amazing co-workers leave due to the dysfunction. My heart has hurt seeing how overworked everyone is in this organization, the number of co-workers having health issues including depression. I've stayed because I learned from an early age to be responsible, which meant to hold a good job with benefits. I went to college for this, and I'm proud of my hard work, but there comes a time when we must see what no longer works for us. My health too has been affected because my spirit feels drained, yet the decision to resign has been painful as well. Thoughts go through my mind about whether I'll be okay financially, what will others think of me, what will I do next. The hamster runs constantly through the days and even while I try to sleep. Knowing this too will cause grief adds to the difficulty of the decision. Deep in my soul, I know the answer, and that answer is to honor myself. It's time I practice what I preach and that is setting a boundary.

As many people expressed, "Being responsible is leaving this job. It's taking care of *you.*" This is what I mean about making sure you have a tribe. These are the people who, in a difficult time, you can sit with. They will believe in you, be honest, and push you to become the best version of yourself. There is more in the world for us and we are the only ones who can make a decision to move toward it. I look forward to what will happen in a few weeks when I close this door and find myself looking at new open doors full of opportunity. Who knows where I might be in life by the time you read this book, but I know it will be a journey filled with joy, laughter, tears, and love. Just as I deserve all that my heart desires, so do you.

To remember our own self-worth and how deserving we are of only the best life has to offer is our first challenge. Knowing the universe has enough for everyone and is watching out for all is important. Choosing boundaries is a way in which we care for our own human form and for our soul.

Reflection:

In what ways do you struggle with setting boundaries?

How do you feel about setting boundaries?

In what areas of your life do you believe you need to set more boundaries?

What changes would you like to make in order to have more of your dreams fulfilled?

BOUNDARIES

Boundaries don't always feel good at first but they are imperative to loving ourselves.

Going Within

*I*n a world that is inundated with solutions surrounding how to "fix" everything, from things in your home, to your car, your health, and even your relationships, we rarely hear advice about going within. Social media, television, and billboards feed our minds with quick fixes so we can get on with our lives. The pharmaceutical industry is constantly capitalizing on our desire to feel better quicker as evidenced by a world that relies heavily on medication for a multitude of health conditions. As a society, we have forgotten that sometimes by disconnecting from the crazy world around us and going within, we can find internal solutions. We all know that by turning off our electronics we can oftentimes reset them and fix whatever problem we are experiencing. What if the same is true for us as humans?

Most of us from a very early age were taught to get up, brush off the dirt, take an aspirin to feel better, and move on. And if we were hurting emotionally, we may have grown up hearing things such as, "Let's go have an ice cream. It will make you feel better." All these "solutions" help us feel better for a quick minute while they cover up the issue at hand. But what happens when we keep using these solutions over and over again because the issues keep reoccurring? We find that our aspirin or other medications, our ice cream, and our dusting ourselves off don't really work that well.

I know this from personal experience. I spent many years of my life looking to others for solutions to what I was feeling inside. I believed that talking to friends and family could help me feel better, but what I found was it was also temporary. Yes, being able to express what was inside helped, and I would never discourage anyone from having safe people to be a listening heart in their lives. But what I found was that there was work for me to do that had nothing to do with another person.

After my divorce, I started seeing a therapist quite regularly to help me process the abrupt change in my life and the pain that accompanied it. At first I found myself pretty frustrated because after a short period of time listening to my "woes" he would put it back on me. He'd ask me what I was doing for myself and how I could help myself. He took the focus away from whatever someone may have done that caused me pain and placed ownership of my feeling better back on me. He helped me move from a victim mentality to a woman who had control over her own life. What I didn't realize until that point is that I had a wealth of wisdom inside of me that I could tap into at any time.

From childhood, we're taught to look outside of our body for answers. This is *not* to say that we should never seek outside advice from others. This *is* to say that we do have many answers inside if we know how to listen. The problem is that our society is filled with a great deal of noise, pressure to do more each day, and to be constantly productive. It's not easy to listen to what's inside. Normally what happens for many of us is we get extremely exhausted, overwhelmed, or sick before we slow down. As we talked about earlier in the book, unless we make time for self-care, we end up with a tank that has run out of fuel. Sometimes we end up stuck in bed, unable to function in our daily life due to illness before we learn the importance of going within.

What exactly does it mean to go within? Going within is trusting in your internal ability to help you find the answers to your own healing. Sometimes the answers you find point to your own innate ability to find healing inside. Other times, your answer is that you do need to rally outside help.

What I have found over the years is that many of our physical issues are actual manifestations of what's going on in our minds. We so often hear stories about unfortunate individuals who have literally worked themselves into a heart attack. Stress over time can lead to a variety of medical issues. Some of these symptoms, not all, can be relieved by eliminating the stress in our lives. This is not to say that diseases can be cured by finding ways to help your stress level but finding your internal strength and connecting with your inner being can definitely improve many circumstances.

So in a world in which we sometimes find it hard to make 10 minutes a day for self-care, how exactly do we find the time to go within? The first thing that's important is to believe in your own intuition and ability to find answers inside. Any new practice takes patience. To make the time, you need to believe taking time away from other things is worth it. You need to believe in yourself, your worth, and your ability to help yourself. It's taken years, but I've gotten to the point that I now know when I'm circling the drain and when to just "stop" before I end up ill. I can listen to what my body is trying to tell me and the red flags it's putting in front of me.

I know so many people who have built up hundreds of hours of sick time, refusing to take a sick day until they become so ill there is absolutely no choice. Although this is an amazing work ethic, I have to question whether that's honoring the body. Sometimes we are just tired. What we truly need is to pause for a day, regroup, and recharge. But if we don't "listen" to our bodies, we will keep pushing on until we have no choice but to slow down. Pushing ourselves to exhaustion is ignoring the red flags our body is trying to send us.

How do we "hear" the messages that will guide us? Everyone has different ways to go within. Some people find that meditation is how they connect with their spirit. They develop a daily practice of meditation either first thing in the morning or before bedtime. For those of us who find it hard to just let things go in our thoughts, it can at times be difficult to meditate. Once I finally stopped beating myself up about the thoughts drifting through my mind while I tried to meditate, I was able to gain clarity from the experience.

Meditation is truly a practice of learning to "let go" which, for many of us, is quite difficult. If you are someone who finds it easier to relax your mind with sound versus silence, there are many wonderful compilations of nature sounds or chanting that can help with meditation practice. I've even challenged myself in the past with a 21-day meditation practice through Mike Dooley, which has brought a wonderful practice into my life. When we do something every day for a period of time, it becomes something that we can more easily adopt into our lives permanently.

Intuition is our inner knowing. When we spend time in meditation or other spiritual practices which bring us to a place of calm, we become more adept at accessing our intuition. Some call it that small, soft voice inside our head that works to help us along the way. It is the red flag that raises when we are in situations that are dangerous to our well-being, and it is the calm voice we hear telling us we will be okay. Intuition does not come from our mind thinking its way through a problem to find a solution. Intuition is always present with a gift if we are quiet enough to hear it. To do this, we must quiet our always-thinking minds. Most of us can hear the warnings if our body is in extreme danger—what's more difficult is to access our intuition for everyday decisions. It takes practice to learn the art of intuition and to believe in what you are hearing.

What I find to be one of the most important ways we can ask for guidance is, "Is this good for me? Does this honor me?" I think it's easy for us to briskly step into situations in our life without first sitting back and allowing our intuition to guide us. Something sounds good, fun, and profitable, but is it really? Split-second decisions often lead us to roads we would rather not travel. Allowing our intuition to guide us helps prevent difficult turns, and later grief, that will weigh us down.

Reflection:

Do you tend to only use your brain to find answers or do you go within and access your intuition?

How might your life benefit if you allowed yourself to be guided more?

In what ways do you connect with guidance within?

_____
_____
_____
_____
_____
_____
_____
_____
_____
_____
_____
_____
_____
_____
_____

GOING WITHIN

There is no situation that cannot be improved by listening to our intuition and internal guidance.

Rest

*I*f you are anything like me, the first couple days of vacation you find yourself unable to really relax. The mind is running in a million directions thinking about what has been left undone and what needs to be done next. As much as you want to be present and enjoy your vacation, you are unable to let go enough for your body to begin to recharge.

Why are we so wired to constantly "do" instead of "be"? Doing leads to productivity, but in the long run, it can also easily lead us into a state of burnout. At that point, we are unable to push ourselves any further and we are forced to rest. Our society has instilled in us that we must always be doing something as evidenced by how many extra-curricular activities we have our children in during the week. And how many do we find ourselves engaged in? Sometimes it feels like we are running from one activity to another until bedtime when we literally collapse onto our sheets.

Remember back to a time in which you were so ill that you had to stay in bed and rest. Physically, you could not "do." You could only "be" in that moment. Your body finally had the last word and put you in a state of having to rest because you were unable to do anything else. You may have pushed yourself so hard, ignoring the whispers and then the red flags that your body was trying to warn you that it was running on empty. We have all been in this position of feeling exhausted yet pushing on until we literally could not push anymore. We were then forced to take a short (or long) rest and begin the vicious cycle again. Unfortunately, most of us are not taught to make a conscious decision to rest before we get to the point of exhaustion.

Often, when we finally either collapse or make a choice to rest, our body's nervous system is so amped up that we are unable to fully embrace resting. I know that I often still find many things to take care of and accomplish, yet wonder why I still feel exhausted. Sometimes we need more than just a little nap to recharge. Sometimes we need days, weeks, or months of rest in which we allow ourselves to "be" and take the focus off of being productive.

The truth is that if we are not whole, well, and healthy in every way, our productivity plummets. Not only does it affect our career but also our relationships as we become so overwhelmed that any little thing tends to set us off. This is our warning sign that it's time to rest.

Slowing down is such a foreign concept for many of us because we pride ourselves on what we can get done on any given day. We have a checklist, and the more things we can check off our list, the better we feel. Does this sound familiar? Imagine how it would feel to have a checklist of ways in which we could care for our own needs. Imagine how much smoother life would run if we put our health before anything else. Most of us do the exact opposite because we were taught that focusing on our own well-being may be selfish. If you believed that your wellness was the top priority, imagine how this might change your life.

I frequently contemplate why, as humans, we find it necessary to push ourselves to exhaustion. Why are we wired to be constantly productive or competitive? I found myself recently physically depleted yet wanted to go on an easy short hike. My brain told me I should only do a mile or so but the path I chose was 5.6 miles. I fought conflicting thoughts in my mind the whole hike. There were the "take it easy, only do a short walk" thoughts. And there were the "come on, you can complete the whole thing, don't be a quitter" thoughts. I could see how the latter has negatively impacted my life at times, pushing me further than my body was physically capable of in the moment. This thinking usually leads to physical and emotional burnout. Knowing this, the question is again, *Why do we let ourselves get to this point?*

Since the beginning of time, men have typically set out to provide for their families by way of hunting while women took care of the children and the home. There wasn't time for rest and relaxation as they were just trying to survive. While we have not lived in these time periods, these values have been passed on for generations. Those of us who put rest as a priority have somehow had it instilled in us, likely from our families, that this is an important part of life in order to be successful. The rest of us have heard we must always be productive and "doing" to be successful, two completely different messages. Most of us have to fight the messages in our heads telling us to keep busy on a frequent basis. We may fear that others will judge us for slowing down and we may also judge ourselves. There's a reason for the phrase, "We are our own worst enemy."

Instead of choosing to be critical, we can always make another choice. We can choose to be gentle with ourselves. We can choose to listen to what our body needs at any given moment, knowing we only receive one in this life. If we don't care for it well, we will suffer from illness. We can choose to put our needs first. This doesn't mean we are neglectful of other things, it means we take care of ourselves first so we can show up and be successful in other areas. The most important thing we can do is to listen to what we need and find a way to honor the request.

How do you know when you need rest?

- When you wake up after a good night of sleep and you're still exhausted, you need rest.

- When you can't imagine doing one more thing after work, you need rest.

- When you are short with your kids and family and just want silence, you need rest.

- When you start developing bizarre physical symptoms that no doctor can explain, you need rest.

- When you constantly feel overwhelmed and have no idea how you will make it through the day, you need rest.

Now, this is not to say that you don't have other needs besides rest, but giving yourself the space to rest can provide clarity on your next steps moving forward.

Most people believe rest can be obtained in a quick nap or a night of sleep, which is not always true. Often, not only your body but also your mind and your soul feel depleted, which all take a bit more rest to heal. This may involve sleeping without an alarm set and allowing yourself to be guided by your own internal alarm clock. Napping during the day when you feel tired may be necessary. Doing minimal activity unless it feels beneficial, like light exercise. Choosing to only spend time with those who help fill your tank versus deplete it further. Spending time in silence or around calming sounds like the ocean, the trees rustling, birds singing. Allowing yourself to let things slide for a bit while you recoup. Choosing to not make any important decisions. Giving yourself a great deal of grace every moment of the day. If you need to lie down because you are tired, that is ok. If you need to not do anything but read a book all day, that is ok. If you don't want to answer your phone because you need silence, that is also ok. There is no recipe for what rest involves as it's individual, but it is learning to just "be" instead of "do" all the time. It's allowing your body, mind, and soul to relax, recharge, and refuel.

Reflection:

If you believed your own wellness was the top priority, how would your life look different?

What does rest look like in your life?

Are there ways in which you would like to allow yourself more time for rest?

_____
_____
_____
_____
_____
_____
_____
_____
_____
_____
_____
_____
_____
_____
_____

REST

Rest is a gift that we give ourselves. Allowing rest is nurturing our existence here on earth.

Honoring Our Relationships

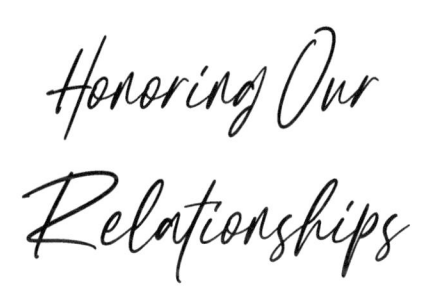

How many of us know how to stay current in our relationships and practice this concept on a regular basis? What does this even mean? Until a few years ago, I had no idea the impact being current in my relationships would have on my own life. I didn't realize that by holding my thoughts, feelings, and emotions inside, I was not only closing my heart to something deeper, but I also wasn't honoring what my relationships have been or the impact they currently have on my journey.

How often do you choose to keep anger, sadness, or even loving emotions inside? Do you find yourself stewing on things, worrying yourself into a place in which you can't think, can't sleep, or have a difficult time concentrating? You may have been taught to keep things inside during your childhood. You may have been told that others don't need to hear everything you are thinking and feeling. Unfortunately, we keep so much from those we love by making this choice. As a result, our relationships start to suffer over time.

Most of us have experienced a significant loss in our past in which we regret not telling someone how we felt. We may regret not clearing up miscommunication, and then it was too late. We may also regret not expressing to someone we care for how much they impacted our life. Some of us may feel embarrassed by expressing emotions and worried about how others will receive our message. I was one of those until I learned the value of staying current in my relationships not only for myself but also for the other person. My Grief Recovery Method work and the healing of my heart have allowed me the insight, wisdom, and courage to show up this way in life.

Not staying current in our relationships and ending up with regrets can have a devastating effect on our lives, one that we carry into future relationships. Regret, in many cases, can keep us stuck in unhealthy patterns and beliefs, which limits our ability to form new, healthy relationships. If we have regrets surrounding the relationships we had/have with our family of origin, these can weigh heavily on our hearts for years or even our lifetime, if not healed. We may think that we have time to heal the strife we've had with others or tell them how much they mean to us, but we are not promised another day. We never know what each day will bring and how that will shape our future positively or negatively. We are always at choice and get to choose how we direct our energy. Even if we choose to no longer engage in a relationship, it is healthy to leave it without words unsaid so that we can move on.

Don't get me wrong, I am in no way perfect. I may have a disagreement and not clear it up right away. And when I make this choice, I can see how my choice is not beneficial to my well-being. I also know that taking a pause and coming back with a more level head goes quite a bit further than the response I may give in a heated moment. Coming back to my heart during a pause allows me to come from a place of love, which is how I choose to navigate my relationships.

Making sure those I care about know they are important to me and I'm grateful for their presence is a choice I make daily so that I won't someday have regrets. I recognize the value of this choice in my life. I also see the value for others as they have someone in their life who chooses to show up with authenticity and love; this is not always experienced by everyone in their own life. Again, it's shining a light for others and empowering them to see their own value.

As I sit here writing tonight, I've resigned from my nursing job and literally have three working days left. My heart has been full of so much gratitude for the ability to see the importance of the gift I've been given and that is to honor all my relationships. My heart hurts for all my co-workers who will be missed. Thankfully, I've had the opportunity to speak with them one-on-one and let them know they are important to me. I've been able to share my gratitude because I've learned the importance of telling people I love what they mean to me. This practice alone brings a great deal of peace into my own life—especially in difficult times. Knowing that I'm complete and current in my relationships is a weight that is lifted off my heart and mind, giving me more energy to invest in important connections with those I love.

Reflection:

In what ways do you hold back from staying current in your own relationships?

What do you know that you need to or want to tell someone that you've been resisting?

Are there relationships you need to get current with in your own life? How will you do this?

_____
_____
_____
_____
_____
_____
_____
_____
_____
_____
_____
_____
_____
_____

HONORING OUR RELATIONSHIPS

Any words left unsaid are thoughts and feelings that keep us from living a life of wellness with fulfilling relationships.

Choosing Vulnerability

When you look up the definition of "vulnerable," you may see words such as "susceptible to physical or emotional harm or attack." Well, honestly, most of us would look at these definitions and run the other way from choosing to be vulnerable. Who wants to be susceptible to harm? No healthy person truly wants to be harmed. When we talk about vulnerability in relationships, we are talking about taking the risk of sharing our weaknesses, emotions, thoughts, and fears. While this definitely does not equate to causing harm, I think it's important to talk about who we choose to be vulnerable with. Most of us don't share our deepest secrets with anyone walking down the street, but instead, choose someone from our tribe, someone we can trust to love us unconditionally and not pass judgment. Absolutely the last thing we want to have happen is to share things which are meaningful to us and have others give negative feedback, use our words against us in a harmful way, or choose to share with others.

Some of us choose to keep most of our feelings bottled up inside without the willingness to share because we think others will judge us. The truly magical thing about being vulnerable with the right people is it draws others closer to us and our relationships deepen. Small talk keeps our relationships surface level, which may be comfortable and seemingly without risk. Most of us desire to have deeper connections, but for us to find this, we must risk being vulnerable.

I remember years ago working at a hospital where I'd walk across a skybridge often seeing the same people. Every day I'd hear the same question, "How are you?" I'd always answer "fine" or "good," and they would do the same. One day it dawned on me that I liked these individuals, but I didn't know them at all because I kept choosing to not really tell them anything about me. How can I be "fine" every day? I can't. I was dishonest and gave them an answer I felt they wanted so that I didn't have to be vulnerable. I was afraid that if I said something like, "It's been a difficult day," they wouldn't care or ask me anything more.

I made up stories in my head about why I shouldn't be vulnerable. And by being vulnerable, I'm not even speaking of deep, dark secrets. I just wasn't willing to share what my current experience was in that specific moment or day. What I found over time was that the more willing I was to show up and be honest about my experience, the more connected I became to those around me. They also shared more about their life, thoughts, and emotions. Our friendships blossomed.

When I first realized I enjoyed writing about my life experiences, I felt afraid every time I would post something on social media. I even thought of specific friends who might have a less than positive reaction to my words or think I was "strange." I came up with all kinds of reasons to not put my thoughts out there even though nothing I wrote was offensive. In reality, I was making excuses to not be vulnerable, to not let others "see" me. What I found was that more often than not, someone would send me a message thanking me for something I wrote, saying it was what they needed that day or they would tell me how it helped them. I started seeing that my vulnerability touched others and did make a difference. I looked back and realized that it was others' vulnerability that encouraged me to also be vulnerable and share with those around me. Again, it's the ripple effect that we create when we are willing to put ourselves out there; it encourages others to do the same.

As I've grown older, I've discovered the value of relationships in which both parties are willing to open up and be vulnerable. I find it boring to constantly talk about superficial topics. I want to know what brings those I love joy, what makes them cry, what dreams they have. I want to know and share the depth of a person because that is what connects all of us here on this earth. Unfortunately, so many souls do not have people in their life that they are able to connect with at this level. I want to encourage you to choose vulnerability with someone you trust and discover the magic it can bring into your relationships.

Reflection:

Do you choose to be vulnerable or do you avoid sharing? If you avoid sharing, why? What are your fears?

Who do you trust enough in your life to be vulnerable with?

Can you choose one relationship in your life in which you would like to be more vulnerable and put this into practice? Come back later and journal about your experience. What went well? Did anything not go well?

_____
_____
_____
_____
_____
_____
_____
_____
_____
_____
_____
_____

CHOOSING VULNERABILITY

How can anyone truly know me if I choose to stay hidden? Isn't it my vulnerability that allows others to see me for who I am?

Being Present

On a recent backpacking trip, I realized how easy it is for me to *not* be present but instead to be thinking about the past or what may be in the future. Having recently left my job and unsure about my path, I figured my head would be in constant deliberation during my trip. Surprisingly, as I was taking my first-ever backpacking trip with my son in the Sawtooth Mountains, I became aware that I was not thinking about what may be. Instead, I fully focused on this new adventure. My only worries revolved around my current experience. *Would the hike be too strenuous? Would I make it to our pre-planned destination?* It was a very free feeling not spending hours contemplating what life would look like in a month or two from now.

By staying in the present with our thoughts, there are two gifts that come about. The first gift is for those we are choosing to spend time with. By being fully present, we give our full attention to others. Instead of taking away from their experience with us by being distracted, we choose to show up fully. Our attention goes to them, which allows a deeper, more sincere connection. The gift of not only our physical but also our mental presence can help us make memories that will be precious to us for years to come.

The second gift of choosing to be present is for us as individuals. Our presence can be felt by others and may encourage them to open their hearts and share with us in ways they may have been hesitant to do in the past. We develop deep connections with others and find that by letting go of thoughts about the future and the past, we are more able to engage in the present moment.

I remember so many times in the past in which I missed out on some special times because I chose to be focused on a situation I couldn't control. The truth is we cannot change the past, and we can't always control the future. What we *can* do is be present *now* to the best of our ability.

Not only does failing to be fully present in the here and now affect our relationships but it also alters the quality of our lives. The universe constantly places things on our path to enrich our lives whether it be individuals, experiences, or signs. When we are distracted with thoughts about the past or future, we often miss what is right in our line of vision.

Some of the things we miss may seem small, like the beauty surrounding us, while others may be quite instrumental in our journey, like an encounter we were meant to have with a stranger. I can't tell you how many times a random conversation with someone I've never seen before changed the trajectory of my life in some way. I wonder how many times I've missed out on those moments because I was caught up in my own thoughts.

Every encounter, whether it be with another person or with our surroundings, shapes who we are as souls on this earth. By making the most of every moment, we enrich our lives.

Reflection:

Do you find yourself in the present moment often or focusing on the past/future?

How may you improve on being more present with others?

What keeps you from being present?

My physical body may be in the room but if my mind is focused somewhere else, my lack of presence will be felt by all. My gift to you is my complete presence when we are together.

Nurture Your Soul In Nature

In my younger years, I lived for about 6 years in Sun Valley, Idaho, hiking, skiing, biking, and spending most of my hours outside. I remember how much I loved watching the aspen trees fluttering in the breeze. There was always such a peaceful feeling that came over me as I watched them rustling and saw the sun glistening through the branches. At the time, I didn't realize the impact that would have on my life. I wasn't aware of the importance of spending time outside in nature. It wasn't until adulthood and after my divorce that I really immersed myself in the outdoors again and recognized the benefits of the experience.

I remember being at work feeling sad shortly after my divorce. My friends were all talking about going hiking over the weekend and encouraged me to join them. After hearing that they were planning a 6-8 mile hike, my words were, "I can't do that." I thought there was no way I could endure that type of walking in nature and certainly not up mountains. Apparently, I'd forgotten my own strength and capabilities. I'd forgotten that in middle school and high school I was a long-distance runner. Obviously, I was in a state of not believing in myself anymore. I had forgotten that at one point, my cross-country class ran 10 miles around a lake and not only did I beat every female but I also beat a great deal of the males. Certainly, I could accomplish this hike my friends were dragging me on, right?

Fast forward to the day of the hike when I felt nervous and apprehensive. As we gathered in the parking lot, I mustered all my strength to make it through the day and not let my friends down as this appeared quite important to them. My friends will never let me forget that shortly into the hike, they were laughing, telling me to slow down because they couldn't keep up. I successfully completed the hike and it started me on my journey of exploring the outdoors as an adult. They love to remind me of the fact that when I struggled to believe in myself, I was actually more than capable.

What I found during this adventure in nature was that my breathing was deeper, my mind was much clearer, and my soul felt at greater peace. The heaviness I was carrying from my recent divorce became lighter. I felt hope and joy, something that had been missing for a long time. I felt excitement as I imagined future hikes in the wilderness and where they might take me.

The sounds of the trees rustling in the breeze, the birds chirping, and the creeks bubbling seemed to calm my soul. The smell of nature, the pine trees, the fresh air, and the spring flowers opened my senses even more. I realized that there is so much more to life than the current heartache I was experiencing. I could see that there were many things going on that I was not noticing as I was stuck in my grief. The universe was showing up for me in amazing ways, but I could only see one thing.

Have you ever stopped to pause and notice how much beauty there is surrounding you that often goes unnoticed? We get so busy in our days that we pass things up. We dismiss the beauty, the love, and those things which can help bring out the best in us. When we are constantly surrounded by computers, TVs, telephones, people, and noise, we can't always see everything that is meant for us. We cannot see the beauty of life, the miracles, because our minds are preoccupied with so many other things vying for our attention. In the example of grief, often all we can see and feel is pain, but there is always so much more if we can step beyond our current state.

There is love. The universe is continually showing up for us either with experiences to help us grow or things to help us heal. Nature is one of those things which can do both in our life. I can't tell you how many times even sitting in my backyard with the trees, flowers, my small garden, and my kitty has lifted my soul and brought me calm. It's not always possible to take a few hours to hit the trails, which is my favorite spirit lifter, but I can always choose to sit in my yard and drop into a peaceful state. When we allow ourselves to see beauty everywhere, we give up the expectations of how we want or think things should be. No, you might not have time to go to your favorite place in the woods or the ocean but what can you do instead? Where is an alternative place to fill up your soul?

Why is the outdoors so important in our healing and our wellbeing? Nature has a distinct energy within it that can counteract the energy of the chaos in our lives. Nature's energy is uplifting, light, loving. Nature is always working toward order so the energy isn't chaotic like our homes and our jobs.

Breathing deeply while outdoors you can feel the sense of peace start to fill your soul and bring more of a sense of calm to your body. I even find that when I'm feeling anxious, which is leading to physical ailments, just spending time in nature restores my balance and brings equilibrium back to my body. There is so much to be learned from nature through all of our senses and when we immerse our human bodies into these environments, we benefit from the gifts.

Reflection:

How do you *feel* when you spend time in nature?

In what ways would spending time in nature benefit you and your life?

What happens to your energy after being in the outdoors?

_____
_____
_____
_____
_____
_____
_____
_____
_____
_____
_____
_____
_____
_____
_____
_____

NURTURE YOUR SOUL IN NATURE

Peace comes from within, but sometimes we need to find a special place that is full of peaceful energy to help us restore ours. Often this place is nature.

Nurture Your Body with Nutrients

One of the things that I find interesting is how, on our most stressful days, we tend to neglect our bodies. These are the times when we may struggle to find even a few moments to exercise, meditate, or eat healthy. We may be running from one meeting or event to another and find ourselves so busy we lack the time to focus on what we are choosing for our body.

Can you remember a time when the only way you felt you could nourish your body in the moment was to find a drive-thru and then eat while you were still driving to your next scheduled stop? There is a reason drive-thru food is called "fast food." It's prepared quickly so you don't have to wait long to consume it. Sadly, it's usually easier to eat unhealthy food than it is to eat healthy foods when we are in a pinch for time. Fortunately, today there are a few healthier options at some drive-thru restaurants but historically that has not been the case.

I can remember all the evenings when my son was young, getting home from work, and feeling exhausted. The last thing I wanted to do was fix dinner, especially anything that took much effort and time. Eating healthy has always been important to me, but I found that when I was tired or felt stressed, I'd resort to more processed foods that didn't provide my body with the same nutrients. It usually didn't take very many days of eating this way before my body would send up some red flags. My exhaustion would get worse, my gastrointestinal system would start to feel bloated and upset. Thankfully, when I took time to look at how I was taking care of my body, I usually realized that what I was putting into it was not helping it thrive. I reminded myself that it was important to nurture my body if I wanted to be able to function at my full capacity.

One thing I didn't allow when my son was growing up were cereals filled with sugar in the morning before school. He knew that he could pick out his own cereal, but it needed to provide a measure of nutrition versus loading him up on simple carbohydrates. We wonder why our children often have trouble concentrating in school after we've fed them sugar without any protein to keep their brains fueled throughout the day. Sugar amps us up, and then we quickly struggle once our body has used its resources without anything additional to burn. The same goes for us as adults; we need to provide adequate nutrition to our bodies throughout the day.

I will share that I am personally one of those people who value my sleep more than getting up extra early to sit and have coffee or tea, read the news, have breakfast, and exercise. I tend to leave myself only enough time to get ready and out the door with not a minute to spare. Even though I've chosen to limit my time in the morning, I still place importance on what I put in my body as I'm starting my day. It only takes five minutes to throw together a smoothie before walking out the door that provides nutrition to fuel your body through the morning. A mix of fruit, nut butter, alternative milk (oat, almond, hemp, coconut), unsweetened yogurt, and spinach or kale provide enough nutrients to jumpstart your day. Even throwing hemp hearts, flax seeds, chia seeds, or other additions into your mixture give it more flavor and added benefits. I know many people who choose to not eat a meal until lunchtime but some of us have difficulty focusing and lose productivity when our body isn't fueled first thing in the morning. Some of us get "hangry" when our tank is running low on fuel, which is never a good way to be effective throughout our day. There are so many different ways to support your body that only take a few minutes to prepare in the morning.

If you look at the current food pyramids/dietary guidelines that focus on plant-based nutrients found in vegetables and fruits, it might cause you to panic. How do I consume all the servings of vegetables that are recommended for ultimate health? Our American diets tend to focus on grains (breads, pasta), meats, and sweets. Many restaurants no longer include salads with their main dishes. Instead, it's an extra cost if you want to order one with your meal. With the price of food right now, most people do not have the extra funds to spend money on anything beyond the basics. If you already don't love vegetables, it can be hard to force yourself to find a place for them in your diet.

When my son was very young, he loved vegetables, but he didn't like lettuce. I found that if I just cut up some of his favorite vegetables, he would eat them willingly, but he refused to eat a salad. I find myself today sometimes using this practice because often it's quicker than preparing a whole salad. It's easy to cut up some carrots, cucumbers, peppers, etc. and throw them in a Ziploc bag to take to work, the gym, hiking. Having these often prevents me from picking up something processed when I find myself needing some fuel throughout the day.

Likewise, there are evenings in which I really don't find I have the energy to prepare a whole meal at the end of the day. Instead of just opening a can of soup or a packaged meal, I might make a plate of cut-up vegetables, cheese, healthy meats, and sometimes crackers or fruits in order to include all the food groups. Even though it's not a fully prepared meal, it provides the nutrition my body needs to fuel itself and it's fairly quick to prepare when I'm pressed for time or lack the energy to create something extravagant.

When we start focusing more on our nutrition and what goes into our bodies, we start to notice that the times when our intake is less nutritious than normal, something doesn't feel right. Our minds don't work as well, our bodies don't feel as well, and our emotions may be all over the place. It's comparable to getting bad gasoline for your car and it not running very smoothly. When we are in our 20s, we might be able to get away with this for a short period of time, but as we age, it becomes more and more important to find the foods/nutrition that help us as a whole feel well.

I think many of us early in our adult life grab whatever food is affordable, quick to access, and provides a sense of comfort. I remember being in college away from home for the first time. I missed home, my family, my friends, and my comforts. Learning how to navigate life independently had its challenges even though I was living in a dorm and food was provided. My friends and I must have ordered pizza four to five times a week, not only because it meant we didn't have to eat the same food from the cafeteria but also because it just felt like a comfort from home. We would stay up late studying, eating pizza, and often run out to Dairy Queen sometime before midnight to get another carb load, a Blizzard. How we all managed to get through college on this diet, I'm not sure. But I do know those times stand out in my memory because they were filled with joy versus the sadness of missing home.

It's important we give ourselves grace when we revert to stress/comfort eating. It's not going to cause harm short term, and sometimes it just helps us get through a day. When we allow this in our life, we don't punish or shame ourselves. Instead, we reward ourselves for the choices we normally make in our life. It's comparable to being on a diet and allowing cheat days. Nothing is sustainable if you are enforcing rules upon yourself at all times. We must allow flexibility, knowing that the majority of the time, we choose those foods that help create a life of wellness.

Reflection:

Do you tend toward foods which provide healing for your body or those which provide comfort?

What foods do you go to when you're stressed/overwhelmed?

What foods help your body feel well?

What small change could you create in your daily food intake which would benefit your body?

_____
_____
_____
_____
_____
_____
_____
_____
_____
_____
_____
_____
_____
_____

*Everything that we choose to allow into our body
creates either wellness or illness over time.*

Healing Power of Animals

From the time I was born, I was surrounded by animals in my home. My Mom is a lover of animals and always had two dogs, mostly golden retrievers. In my early years, I found them to be my friends, someone to play with and snuggle up next to on the couch. In my adult years, I realized how powerful the loving energy of animals is in our own healing and growth.

Years ago, during a particularly hard time in my life, I was at home working outside in the yard. As I was kneeling down pulling weeds, all of a sudden a tabby cat ran across the street and plopped herself in my lap. Now, I had never been a cat person since I'd always grown up around dogs, so I felt quite surprised with this behavior. I sat with her for a couple minutes and then got up to walk into the backyard to continue my outside work. To my surprise, she followed me into the backyard and everywhere I went. At one point I decided to go inside as it was a hot day and I wanted to sit down for a few minutes out of the sun. This cat who came out of nowhere managed to follow me in the house, ran upstairs, and plopped herself on my bed. I literally did not know what to do. I remember calling my Mom and feeling anxious about what I should do. She suggested I offer her a little bit of tuna in case she might be hungry. Well, little did I know but this would turn into the start of a wonderful journey for the two of us.

Since I wasn't aware of whether this cat had a home, I put it back outside but she just kept showing up each and every day. I finally realized she didn't seem to have a home, but I was getting ready to leave for a trip. I placed a kitty house on my front porch with some food and water thinking when I came home, she would be gone. To my surprise, she was still at my house waiting to greet me with love and snuggles. It was at that point I knew our home now had a kitty to call its own.

My son quickly became attached to our sweet little tabby who we named Faith. Faith seemed like a perfect name as she appeared in a particularly painful time in my life and provided me with faith that things would get better. Her constant love for both of us lifted the energy in our life in ways I hadn't realized could happen. She made us smile, laugh, and find joy in the simple things. She gave us something to look forward to every time we came home from work and school. She literally changed our lives.

Fast forward to today. Faith is now 16 years old and has seen us through some difficult years. Although she herself has some health issues, she enjoys her daily time outside, eating her favorite snacks, and snuggling up with her humans. She's been a constant comfort during the years of being at home due to COVID, and she has given us so much joy in her senior years. The past few years, I've really grown to realize how much an animal's presence adds to the quality of our lives.

What is it about animals that has a healing effect on us as humans? Animals have this innate ability to sense our needs as well as provide that unconditional love that is more difficult for us as humans to express. We can rely on them to always be there for us (although cats can be a bit selfish at times). Their whole existence revolves around being our companions. They want to be close and don't hold grudges like we humans often choose to do. We may be gone on a trip for the week, but it won't be long after we return that they've forgotten about our absence and act as if nothing has changed. I think for most of us, it's easier to form a strong connection with an animal than it is a human because of many of these characteristics. We may not hold the same fear that they will leave us as we do for humans. We understand that they will be with us until they are no longer on this earth which allows us to open our hearts wider for them.

I believe animals teach us how to love in many ways. We often hold our fellow humans to an expectation that they should not do anything to hurt us. As we know, it's impossible to never hurt another human because we are human. We all experience days in which we are far from that love and light we desire. We may lash out with our words or our behaviors in ways in which we are ashamed of in the future. Somehow it is easier to not hold our animals to that same expectation. They may growl and snarl and ignore us on occasion but for the majority of the time, they are loving and wanting to be close. For those of us with animals, we understand and feel the healing of their energy.

There are many who believe that a cat's purring has a healing effect on the human body. I'm not sure whether or not this is scientifically proven to be true. I do know that when I'm ill, Faith likes to lie either on my chest or right next to me. The majority of the time, I notice a shift in my energy and symptoms, which leads me to believe these reports to be true. Perhaps it's just her love that is healing, but whatever it is, I find myself wanting to have her close by and look forward to seeing her at the end of my day. She continually provides a great deal of light and love to our lives.

Reflection:

If you have a pet, how do you find it helps you in your life?

Does your heart feel as open for humans as it does for your pet?

May your unconditional love for animals be also found in your love for humans in the remembering that we are all one.

Choices

Choices! Can you imagine what life would look like if we didn't have a choice? If our life was pre-set and we had no influence on our path, it would certainly look quite a bit different than it does today. As hard as it is to sometimes make a choice, I remind myself often how grateful I am to have the ability to shape my time here on earth. Knowing if one path doesn't take me in the direction I'm desiring, I can choose another brings a great deal of comfort to me. Despite the gratitude, I recognize that it's not always easy to have a choice. We may think it would be easier if there were none, but look at the magnificent life we can experience if we choose certain paths. Our opportunities are endless. Each one of us can make a conscious decision to use what time we have on earth to live life to the fullest.

If you are like me, you struggle at times with being pulled among multiple things, trying to make a difficult choice. It's during these times when my head and heart are competing, trying to outrun one another and neither wanting to be defeated. Unfortunately, one must win out. Usually it's the one that makes the most sense from an integrated head and heart perspective.

There are definitely moments we just want to jump into something or out of something because that's what our heart is telling us to do. For most of us, though, we choose to also involve our head because we are not used to living strictly from our heart or trusting it will lead us in the right direction. There also may be many variables involved to contemplate, especially if we are faced with a big life choice. Quitting a job or leaving a relationship, for example, come with multiple facets which need to be considered.

The universe may be throwing an abundance of signs your way, telling you it's time to move on from your job. Perhaps it's depleting your soul and not honoring the gifts you come with in this world. However, most of us need to determine what our next step would be prior to making a decision of this magnitude. Do I have another job lined up or enough money to sustain me until I figure out the next step? If I'm not going to another benefited position, what will I do about benefits? These are all important questions to consider.

Likewise, when leaving a relationship, you may know it's the right thing for you to do but what comes with this decision? Will you need to find another place to live? How will this affect other areas of your life, such as family, career, etc.? Making these decisions can be something that takes a great deal of time and consideration but also courage. How do we know when we are making the best decision in the moment?

I trust that the universe guides us to that which is for our highest good. However, I also know that my head gets involved and tends to stall the choices I make. I know that once my head lines up with my heart that my decision is one that is going to lead me to something better. That doesn't mean it's not scary, because change tends to be anxiety-producing, but it means that my soul knows taking a leap is the right thing for me at this time. Allowing my intuition to guide me is important when making life changes. Learning to trust what the future will look like definitely takes some practice.

When making a choice to leave my nursing job recently, I spent months (if not years) saying I needed to quit, only to keep showing up every day. My heart knew leaving was the right choice for me. My physical and mental health was being affected, my soul felt like it was being sucked dry and I was not enjoying my life. But my head got involved, causing me to worry about what would happen if I left.

What will I do for money and benefits?

What will my life look like?

Will others support my decision?

Will I ever go back to nursing?

Will I find something else to do?

I spent many sleepless nights contemplating all of this until one day I just couldn't do it anymore. It became increasingly clear that my organization did not support its employees or value them in the way they deserved. I realized that if I continued, my health would continue to be negatively affected and my soul would feel as if it was slowly dying. As soon as I made the choice to do something different, life changed for me. My stress level decreased dramatically, my sleep improved, and my soul felt true joy again. This told me that the choice I made was the right one for me at this time. I know that by following the signs that the universe uses to guide me, life will bring me to the places I am meant to be. I remind myself, "You need not worry about your future."

Reflection:

What choices are you struggling with right now?

What is your heart saying about your choices versus what is your head saying?

Do you tend to listen more to your head or your heart?

_____
_____
_____
_____
_____
_____
_____
_____
_____
_____
_____
_____
_____
_____
_____
_____

CHOICES

One choice today can put your life on a whole new path. Taking one small step forward may open doors into the future of your dreams.

Grace

Are you someone who often has a great deal of compassion for others but tends to be hard on yourself? Do you have higher expectations for yourself than those around you? I often listen to those I love beating themselves up verbally for a variety of things. For example, not being strong all the time, having bad days in which one isn't able to be there for others, or being downright cranky. If you have someone in your life who is perfect every minute of every day, let me know. I certainly don't. I believe perfection means being perfectly imperfect.

When we hold ourselves to such high standards that we can't meet them, it chips away at our self-esteem. It's impossible to show up as love and light every single moment of every single day. We are human. We have feelings. We get hurt. We have bad days. We sometimes wake up on the wrong side of the bed. All of it is okay—and normal. But what do most of us do with it? We tell ourselves we should do better or feel guilty. We need not feel guilty when we didn't mean to cause harm to another.

Giving ourselves grace means we always do our best but understand that we all have difficult, trying days in which we may not live up to our own expectations. Instead of making things worse by beating ourselves up, we choose to be gentle and focus on what we need in the moment. We may need to pause and take some time to recharge if we've become overwhelmed or unable to function at our full capacity. Maybe it's time to spend some time in nature, meditate, nurture our bodies, and find that special place which helps us get centered.

When our life feels like it's spinning out of control, remembering the rituals we can do that bring us back to center is imperative for us finding that peace and calm again. If we continue doing what we've been doing, we will lack the energy to perform at our best. We will create the cycle of disappointment. Stepping back and taking a break is sometimes the healthiest and most graceful thing we can do during these times. This doesn't mean we "can't" handle our life or we aren't capable. This means we, like everyone else, need a pause sometimes so that we can come back rejuvenated. This pause helps us create a healthy life and healthy relationships moving forward.

There are also days in which even taking a step forward to engage in our usual rituals that bring us back to center seems absolutely out of reach. We may feel under the weather physically or emotionally. We may be grieving a loss or just feel exhausted. In the back of our minds, we may be telling ourselves to exercise, meditate, connect with others, drink more water, or eat healthy foods, but the only thing we feel capable of is getting out of bed. This is okay. We don't need to always live up to the standards we have set for ourselves. We can have down days and still be extremely successful. The important piece is to make whatever we are experiencing okay and not try to force something. If we are curled up in bed for days at a time, isolated from the world, that is a completely different situation. Those situations often require assistance of other professionals. But what I am talking about is those "off" days in which we don't feel like doing a dang thing. We may not know why we lack motivation or feel "not right" but once again offer grace.

Sadly, we often expect to constantly be productive or pushing ourselves. We may think less of ourselves for having an off day and mull over in our mind for hours what may be "wrong" with us.

How about we love who we are?

What if we don't view these days as if we've failed?

Why don't we stop believing there's something faulty about us?

What if we looked at these moments and days as normal occurrences?

Why not take a break, pause, and be quiet?

Imagine how much less time we would focus on what we perceive as our shortcomings. Instead, we can allow ourselves to rest so that tomorrow we are even more productive.

For some of us who don't sleep well on a nightly basis, we get to the point of pretty much being forced to rest. Sleep is normally when our body heals and rejuvenates. Without adequate sleep, our nervous system is constantly firing without the rest it needs to take care of even the smallest cellular structures. Not only do our organs suffer but our brains also no longer work in the same way. Our thoughts may be affected leading to decisions and actions that may not benefit our lives in the future. If we don't take time to rest when our bodies speak up, we are not honoring the amazing machine that keeps us going every day. We absolutely must listen to those small whisperings from the inside that tell us we need rest. We need to allow rest to be something we encourage versus push against. Having grace with yourself means honoring what you need at any given moment. In doing this we support our body, mind and spirit in everyday life.

Reflection:

What does it mean to you to give yourself grace?

Historically, have you had grace for yourself or have you held yourself to a different standard than you do others?

List two ways in which you can show yourself greater compassion.

GRACE

If we cannot be graceful with ourselves first, we cannot fully offer this to others. One must first embody this compassion toward oneself.

Accepting Your Present Reality

For those of us who strive to bring light into the world around us, we may struggle during those times when we have difficulty bringing forth our own light. Perhaps we hold ourselves to high standards and when we are not able to meet them, we feel as though we are letting others down. As we discussed earlier, it's extremely important to remember that we need not be perfect. It is our imperfections that bring more depth into our experience. Choosing to be transparent with others about our current experience encourages others to do the same.

Often when we come forth with our own story, willing to be vulnerable, it's actually what encourages others to do the same. Life isn't all unicorns and rainbows. Life has its ups and downs, and to share those is to be real and human. Even though we want to present ourselves in the best light, sometimes it's not possible, which is important for us to accept.

Recently, I reconnected with a friend whom I hadn't seen in over a year. This is someone I greatly admire as being around her feels like sunshine. She's not only kind but also uplifting and empowering. Most importantly, she's honest. Within moments of reconnecting, she chose to share some really difficult things she'd been experiencing in the past few months and how she was feeling about herself. Instead of having just a "nicey nice" conversation, she accepted her reality and put it out for me to listen. This acceptance of herself led to further connection and compassion from me. All I could see when she was sharing was a beautiful soul navigating life. I didn't see failure or think anything less of her in the moment.

We tend to be really hard on ourselves. We expect perfection, but that's not attainable. Understanding that where we are in the present moment is okay gives us the ability to navigate difficult times in our lives without added pain. If we are already hurting, the last thing we need is to be beating ourselves up about not living up to our standards. Offering grace to our humanness allows us to see beyond our own disappointments. We always have the ability to apologize if we feel that we've done wrong to another. Apologies are often not expressed, so when we hear one, it's such a gift that most embrace.

There will be days, weeks, and sometimes months that we feel off. We may have difficulty being the light we desire and may only be able to do the basics. Getting out of bed, going to work, and taking care of your family may seem like daunting tasks. You may feel worn out, depleted, and depressed. It's as if you are just going through the motions. I get it. I've been there. And these are the times we often need to focus on our own self-care, which includes self-love. Our focus turns from an external focus to an internal one. We focus on being a light for ourselves or at the least acceptance and love. We allow ourselves time to recharge and get back to the person we want to show to the world. This may mean we need to become more introverted while we take care of our wellness and spirit. Maybe this looks like quiet time, meditation, reading, or sleep. It could be time in nature or a trip alone. Do whatever you need to do to recapture your essence in your present experience. The important thing is to love yourself as you accept where you are in the present moment.

Reflection:

How can you be more accepting of your present experience? What would that look like for you?

_____
_____
_____
_____
_____
_____
_____
_____
_____
_____
_____
_____
_____
_____
_____
_____
_____
_____
_____

Acceptance of our current experience allows us to move through it with greater ease.

Solitude

I remember one time talking to some of my friends about my upcoming trip to Sedona. Every single one of them asked me who I was traveling with and my answer was always the same, "myself." I received some strange looks followed by questions about why would I want to travel alone. Wouldn't I be lonely or bored? When my answer was that I love to travel by myself because it helps me disconnect from the world and reconnect to myself, only some understood. And when I explained that traveling by myself always led to great adventures and meeting really interesting people, which likely wouldn't happen if I had a travel partner, I could tell thoughts were swirling through their heads.

After my divorce, I realized the value of solitude. Sometimes this alone time was at home, other times it was in another country, another town, or in the woods. I found that it was in these quiet moments—with no looming expectations from others or need to communicate—that I was able to allow my body and mind to rest. Our world is so full of noise and chatter that sometimes it's hard to even think. Drowning out the constant noise isn't always possible when we're around others. We are inundated at work, home, school, stores, and cars with noise from voices and electronics. We now have "voices" who talk to us on all of our electronics if we so choose. It's no longer easy to be surrounded by silence unless we seek it out.

I remember landing in the Miami airport to go through customs after one of my international missions. The first thing I noticed was the loud TVs with advertisements for everything you might ever need but more like everything you would ever want. It was absolutely overwhelming when I had just come from two weeks in a rural area which had little in resources yet functioned just fine and especially without the level of noise we are inundated with daily in the states.

We get so used to being surrounded by noise that it's "normal" and we may not see that there is a need for any other way. However, our brains get short-circuited when hundreds of things are being constantly thrown at us to process. Although our brains are amazing organs, they still cannot focus on every single thing that's happening around us at all times. Our focus always goes somewhere. Unfortunately, when we are overwhelmed, that focus tends to pull us away from self-care, which is why it's important to remind ourselves to step back and find space to be alone and quiet.

Some may have difficulty with absolute quiet and feel anxious as their minds swirl with thoughts. I've often found it effective when I take time for myself to listen to some soft, relaxing sounds like the ocean, trees, birds, or something in nature. The sounds need to be soothing and not something that will raise your heart rate, create more stress, or bring up anxiety-producing thoughts and memories.

There is not a right or wrong way to spend your time alone. The important thing is to create this space and then honor what you need in the moment. Sometimes you may need a nap, other times to read a book or meditate. Then there are the times a walk in nature will help connect you to your heart again. I know that when I'm needing time alone, I start to feel a restriction in my breathing, which is a sign that I'm not connected to myself. Usually this is because I'm too focused on the overwhelm I feel in my life. There are times when I don't pay attention to that first sign, and the universe has to deliver a few before getting me to take notice. When this happens, I remind myself to accept that I'm doing the best I can in this given moment. The important thing is that we do honor the sacredness of our alone time when we create it. We recognize that this precious time is a gift we give ourselves. In turn, we fill back up and can then provide light for those around us.

Reflection:

How do you feel about being alone? Is it something that produces anxiety or is it welcome?

Talk about a time when you were alone and what you encountered in the experience.

What benefits have you experienced in the past from spending time alone?

Would you like to create more experiences of being alone? How do you feel this will increase your sense of well-being?

_____
_____
_____
_____
_____
_____
_____
_____
_____
_____
_____
_____

We first have to learn to be good with ourselves before we can be good with others.

Have Faith

I've never been a deeply religious person, but that doesn't mean I don't believe in something larger than myself. I find my beliefs more spiritual in nature as I identify with a higher power, but in my mind, that higher power doesn't require a specific identity. It's not necessary for me to follow any specific religion. Instead, I follow the principles of kindness, compassion, integrity, honesty, and love. I respect the beliefs of those around me and allow others to follow their own life path, whatever that may be.

As we all know, life has its rollercoasters to endure. Although we would like for it to be all smooth sailing, the truth is that we often feel as though we are climbing a mountain. There have been times in my life when I have felt very alone. This was not because I was physically alone, it was because I had lost my own faith. Feeling stuck and depressed, I almost found myself not wanting to believe there was something more in the universe guiding our lives, which only led to more suffering for me. It wasn't until I could put myself into a place of "remembrance" that I would find my way back to faith. Once my faith was restored, I could feel the presence of something greater than myself again, something to help guide and protect me on my journey.

I certainly never tell others what to believe or not believe. As I stated previously, I allow others to find their own path to follow. I do believe, though, that it's important we carry faith with us. It really doesn't matter to me how that faith looks just that we all have it to help us through this life. As long as our faith has a foundation of kindness and love, we are putting out healing energy into the world.

Why is it so important that we believe in something greater than ourselves? These beliefs help us in our most difficult times. They help us see that there is more to our life and that things will change just like the seasons. It helps us see beyond our own suffering. These beliefs can bring us community, which provides more support around us. For those who practice some sort of religion, there is often a congregation at a church or designated site allowing individuals to come together. This is important as most of us yearn for that connection in our lives. Whether you practice organized religion or hold your own spiritual beliefs, you can find like-minded individuals to connect with, people who may become part of your own tribe. These individuals can be important in your life, to lean on during difficult times and to cheer you on during good times.

As I talk about having faith in something greater than your own being, I would be negligent if I didn't address having faith in yourself. Without faith in *you* it's difficult to create the life you deserve. Believing in your strength, courage, and ability to do anything you set your mind to is paramount because without this, you will certainly stay stuck in repeated patterns and lifestyles.

Years ago, I made a page on Facebook called "To Believe in You" for the single purpose of helping empower others to believe in themselves and what they can achieve. So often society cuts us down or we are told we are not enough. These repeated messages over time severely affect our self-esteem and often keep us from moving forward with our dreams. We often stay small because we lack that faith in our own wisdom and abilities. I personally believe it's impossible to wake up every day and feel empowered. We all go through rough times, but if we can get up most days and know we are capable, worthy, and important, that mindset will take us in the direction of the things which we desire. Give yourself grace on the rough days and celebrate you on the rest of the days. You are here for a purpose. Remember to have faith in something greater than you, guiding your journey, and faith in your ability to carry out the journey.

Reflection:

How does your faith in something greater than yourself guide your life?

How do you honor your faith? What does it mean to you?

Do you consistently have faith in yourself? If not, what prevents you?

In what ways might you be able to increase your faith to help you create the life you desire?

_____
_____
_____
_____
_____
_____
_____
_____
_____
_____
_____
_____
_____
_____

HAVE FAITH

For it is our faith that guides our life and without it, we often feel stuck somewhere that we are no longer meant to be. Find your faith and you often find your dreams.

Gratitude

"The things you take for granted, others are praying for." What a profound statement. It leads to a great deal of introspection. Think about the things in your life that you may assume will always be present, then realize that others may be lacking these in their experience. This can be quite humbling. It gives one pause to truly be present and grateful in each and every moment.

Most of us wake up every morning, get a cup of coffee or tea, have breakfast, and jump in the shower before starting our day. We have a soft bed to sleep in, running water, and a way to heat up not only water but also food in our homes. Sit back and consider that there are people all over the world who are without any of these conveniences. Imagine the struggle life might be without these things we consider basic necessities. I find myself feeling a deep sense of gratitude when I ponder this instead of just taking them all for granted.

What about family and friends? How easy it is at times to assume they will always be around and in our lives. Reality is, that is not the case. Think back to those who have left our physical world and feel into your desire to perhaps have one last conversation with them or share another special moment to hold dear in your memory. What about your best friend from childhood who you lost contact with? How about your coworker who moved? Most of us feel comfortable with the thought that those we love will be ever present in our lives because we fail to stop and consider that it may not be the case. We get busy in our lives with work, family, friends, and responsibilities. Days pass, and we often forget to make time to really connect with those we love. Even in our own families, we may be pushing through each day without really pausing to appreciate the moments we have with one another. There is often so much we are missing out on when we are just going through the motions.

There are situations that help us to see what is most important and bring us back to a state of gratitude. The pandemic was one of those situations for me. It gave me an opportunity to re-evaluate my life. It clearly showed me who was part of my tribe and where I wanted to invest my time. I remember in the first year, feeling a deep sense of sadness, missing so many people that I loved to spend time with. Once I was able to see them again, even 10 minutes in person felt like a huge gift. In the past, I would have thought that 10 minutes might not be worth it, wasn't enough, but I found myself feeling grateful for each and every minute I could connect one on one in person with those I love. Zoom was a great avenue to connect while we were all home isolating, but over time, it lacked the connection that is possible when you can stand in front of another person, feel their energy, look them in the eyes, and embrace.

Through the pandemic there were chances I took, like getting on a plane to see my son, because it deeply mattered to me. I chose carefully as I realized that there were things I wasn't willing to give up for fear of what may happen. I also began to realize the things in my life that were detrimental to my well-being and began making different choices. I'm a creature of habit, so change is often very difficult for me. However, continuing in a job that was literally sucking my soul dry was no longer sustainable. Realizing that life is short and I want to live rather than exist helped me make a choice to do something different. Without my tribe's support and cheering from the sidelines, I may have struggled more with my decision. These are all moments when I find a great deal of gratitude. I also realize that I am lucky as so many others are lacking things which I am surrounded by in my current experience, including an amazing support system.

As an adult, I've come to cherish Thanksgiving as one of my favorite holidays to spend with those I love. Our family has a long-standing tradition of taking time during dinner to listen and acknowledge each person joining us, what they are grateful for, and choose to share. I find myself feeling full of a great deal of love and joy when I not only reflect on my gratitude but also have the opportunity to hear what others give thanks for on the holiday. Thanksgiving is always a reminder to me of the importance of focusing on the good in life.

Let's be honest, we all go through very trying moments, days, weeks, months, and even years when we have a difficult time recognizing the beauty in our lives. I've personally had moments when others tried to point out the good in my life and I refused to see it because I was in a sea of grief, anger, sadness, or disappointment. Even if we can't see or recognize the universe in support of our journey, it's always showing up in some way.

I've come to realize that life doesn't have to be wonderful to be full of good things. Some days just acknowledging that we are alive and breathing or that we made it through another day is enough. Other days we can feel gratitude for having a roof over our heads, a job, a family, and beautiful friends. It is absolutely possible to recognize what we feel thankful for and still be experiencing a rough day or time in our life. It's often on my hardest days that I practice an evening ritual of recognizing three things I'm thankful for prior to closing my eyes. Most of the time, my ritual is done silently in my head, but it's even more powerful to share these moments with others. It encourages thoughtful awareness of what beauty is a part of our life.

I find that by practicing some type of ritual in which I focus on gratitude, I notice more to be grateful for around me. Positive thoughts attract more beauty into our energy field and give us strength in difficult times. There is so much in our world to be thankful for—even in the midst of chaos, war, devastation, and loss. We can have both at the same time. We can feel sad for the pain around us and feel happy for all that is good. We do not need to choose one or the other.

Reflection:

Take a moment to journal about those things you are grateful for today. List at least three if you can. Now, continue this practice daily for the next week and then reflect on how you feel at the end. What differences do you notice in your life?

GRATITUDE

At times, we may have a hard time seeing it, but there is always something to be grateful for.

Find the Gift

In the introduction to this book, I talked about struggle being a gift. Of course, when I first heard this, I completely disagreed and dismissed the whole idea. It wasn't until years later that I could truly see what the universe had planned for me all along. It had been easier to resist change and believe that I was a victim versus understanding that there's a purpose for our pain and struggle. My egocentric brain found it difficult to wrap my mind around events holding a different purpose from what they obviously appeared to mean in the moment.

Becoming a single, divorced mother at the age of 30 was definitely not in the cards I had planned for my life. There wasn't one cell in my body that could find a gift in all the loss I was experiencing during that time. I was angry, bitter, and felt like a victim. Healing and growth allowed me to finally see how the universe had my back and had so many plans for my life. I realized that if my husband hadn't left me, I would have never opened myself up to finding more of my inner light. I would have stayed small. Although being a mother, nurse, and wife are beautiful gifts, I was also meant to find myself. Growing up in an alcoholic family, I'd mainly tried to fit in to keep the peace. Unfortunately, keeping the peace and fitting in did not lead me to exploring my world and becoming my own person. My divorce, as well as every other loss in my life, gave me this opportunity.

With advancing age, increased wisdom, and the desire to understand life differently, I began to see how the universe was in support of my dreams. I could see how often things were removed from my life. Doors were closed to make room for things that allowed for more growth. It wasn't that life became "easier" with any change. Life just presented me with more opportunities for learning and expansion. I realized we aren't on this earth to stay stagnant. Our souls want to grow, but this only happens when the soul is presented with opportunities that encourage growth.

Of course, everything I just said sounds great on paper, but when your life feels like it's one struggle after another and you are tired, the last thing most of us think about is how wonderful it is to be in our current experience. The exact words that have come out of my mouth multiple times are: "I'm tired of the lessons and the growing." Sometimes we just want easy, flowing lives without a bunch of bumps in the road. I get it! *And,* our purpose on earth is to grow. It's okay to resist this at times and allow yourself to fully grieve painful events and experiences that come your way. Most of us find it hard to live in a peaceful zen state every day. I'm guessing even Buddhist monks have difficulty maintaining this state at all times. Our lives are complicated and unpredictable. Even though we can control our own thoughts, reactions, and emotions, we have absolutely no control over the outside world.

While the world is swirling around us and out of our control, we are often impacted by it in ways that we had not planned. It can lead to us feeling lost, stuck, and heartbroken. Again, there is usually a bigger plan which we are not aware of in the moment. I try to pause and ask myself, "What is this here to teach me?" Sometimes my mind responds with a snarky answer, but more often than not, my intuition kicks in and helps me understand my experience. I cannot stress enough the value of learning to tune into your intuition, your inner self. The answers it provides are not from a place of fear but from a place of love in support of your journey. It helps us find the gifts in our experience when it's otherwise difficult for us to see them. It assures us we are on the right path and supported in our lives. I often realize that experiences I go through have a lesson for me that, if I'm honest with myself, really help my soul grow and become more aligned with my true being, that of love.

Reflection:

Think about a struggle in your current experience. Sit quietly. Meditate if that feels right. Ask your inner self, "What is this here to teach me?" If nothing comes, allow that to be okay and perhaps try again later. If you do hear an answer, does it feel like it's coming from your ego or your intuition? What do you hear and how does this help you move through your current experience?

Feel free to look back through your past and use the same question. Allow your intuition to provide insight into some of your life experiences. Are you able to see the gifts?

_____
_____
_____
_____
_____
_____
_____
_____
_____
_____
_____
_____

Life has a purpose and that purpose is to grow. We are not meant to be stagnant as humans. We are constantly presented with opportunities to help us return to our divine state, a state of pure love.

Love without Measure

We all know someone who walks through life with a glow that emanates constant love. I'm sure many of us wonder how they are able to persist in this angelic state. Now, this isn't to say that when home in their own private space, they may not emit the same level of light. We all have our "off" days, but some of us manage to project love when we are around others. You can see the way some people interact and feel the love genuinely coming from their hearts.

Most of us unfortunately have some walls up around our hearts due to being hurt in the past. We feel somewhat reserved in our expressions of love. We may be worried about how we are viewed by others if we extend love. It's a pure joy to watch someone who has an open heart share it with the world, including strangers. These individuals truly understand the ripple effect—how touching one life ends up impacting hundreds of thousands. There is really no way to know how far the waves of love can spread.

What does it mean to show love? Kindness is love. Compassion is love. Listening is love. Empathy is love. There are so many ways we can show love to those around us. We don't have to know someone to show love. We can extend love to a stranger walking down the street with our smile. We can stop and talk to someone or make time to listen. We can provide a hug.

When we love without measure, we extend the love in our hearts out into the world without concern about where it's spread, to whom, how much, or if it's reciprocated. There is no measuring, there is only giving. And in this giving, the love returns to us in significant ways. Our lives are touched by the love we extend to others. Think about how beneficial that would be for any of us, especially when we are hurting and it's incredibly difficult to open our hearts.

I remember back to my mission trips when we provided surgery to children in underdeveloped countries. Some of these children had never been seen by a doctor in their entire lives. Families walked for miles, and sometimes days, to get care for those they loved. They were often scared, but they managed to put their trust in our medical team, knowing we would provide the needed care for their child's issues. They extended words and gestures of gratitude to our whole team, often bringing us small gifts of their appreciation. Families with so little to take care of their own were willing to give to others from their heart. They didn't spend time focusing on what was missing in their lives but focused on what they did have and how they could share it with others.

On every one of these trips, I felt a great outpouring of love from my heart. These missions were an act of love above all else. And from this love came transformation for these families as their children could now lead more normal lives after having their cleft lips and palates repaired. I gave my time, my nursing skills, and my heart. I ended up feeling all the love I shared coming back to me tenfold on these trips. I was tired at the end of the mission, but I always felt full in my heart. There was never a measure of how much love I was giving. I shared as much as I could possibly share. It was a beautiful exchange. This is what I'm talking about when I use the phrase "love without measure."

We don't need to wait for others to extend kindness and love our way. We can be the one to show up and allow our heart to open. It's not about what we are getting in return, as many times, our love is not returned. It's about what we can give and allowing others to perhaps be touched by our light and love. We all have something to give and to share. We all make a difference by how we show up in the world. I encourage you to think about the difference you want to make. Consider the ways you can show up that allow your heart to be open for others to see.

Reflection:

Reflect back to a time when you remember loving without measure. What were the circumstances? How did you feel giving from an open heart? How did you feel afterward? What effect did it have on your life?

What are some ways that you can create ripples of love around you? What actions are you willing to take?

LOVE WITHOUT MEASURE

*If there is only one thing you do each day,
spread love.*

Be the Change

Years ago, while attending a conference, I listened to a speaker talk about how pain ripples out in the world. He said, "Hurt people hurt people." Wow, what a profoundly true statement. How often do we see someone who is hurting lash out at another? And then that person lashes out at someone else. It's a vicious cycle that ends up spreading more pain versus love and compassion. If only we understood how our own grief hurts others. If only we could remember when others were being less than loving toward us that they are hurting and not react ourselves. But we are all human. None of us want to hurt, nor do most of us want to intentionally hurt others, but sometimes it happens.

I remember a time when a good friend of mine who often came to me for a listening ear was in a very hard space. She was experiencing a great deal of loss in her life, some old and some new. In many ways, she was starting to spiral in a way that was pushing people away. I remember how hurt I was when she started attacking me about asking another friend to watch my kitty while I was away. Her words were hurtful and went straight to my heart. At that time, I wasn't able to see beyond her anger to the deep hurt she was experiencing over other events in her life. I took it personally, reacted, and unfortunately, we did not speak for months. I look back on that time and now realize that if I had stepped back and understood that her pain wasn't at all about me, the situation would have unfolded differently.

We are always at choice. We can choose to respond or to react to another individual. We can choose to rise above the hurtful actions and words of others to help make a change. We can be the change. This is not an easy task as we are wired to defend ourselves when we feel attacked. We are hurting, and often it feels like the only thing to do is attack our attacker. There is another way, but we have to be very mindful and intentional about our actions.

Choosing to pause when another human has hurt us gives us time to thoughtfully choose a response, if any, versus instantly reacting out of anger and pain. The pause gives us space to think about how we want to show up. Most of us want to be that light, offering compassion to others. Most of us do not want to join those who choose out of their own pain to be hurtful toward those around them. When we find ourselves reacting in a hurtful way, we often cause more pain because we then grieve our own behavior that was less than we had hoped for. When we show up in a way that doesn't honor our own light, we end up disappointed in our actions.

I can think back to so many times in my own life when someone treated me poorly, talked behind my back, or lashed out. Sadly, I didn't always have the skills to pause and deeply think about the path I wanted to take. There have been times I've been defensive and hurtful in return. And the older I've become, the more I've learned to differentiate between someone purposefully trying to cause me harm and someone who is hurting inside who doesn't know how to manage the pain. Being able to see another's pain and not react to it not only helps us in our growth and healing but can also plant a seed in others and perhaps lead them onto a path of healing. We don't need to allow abuse from others, we can walk away without a response. We can be compassionate but take care of ourselves first. We can focus on how we choose to show up in the world and be the change we want to see. All change starts with us first. With this in mind, what change would you like to see in the world around you?

Reflection:

When others are hurting and lashing out, how do you typically respond? Does your response/reaction honor you?

What changes could you make in the way you respond to others? How might this benefit your life?

BE THE CHANGE

Change always starts with ME.

Believe In You

I've felt for years that the messages we tend to pass on and share with others are often the messages we also need to hear the most. We will daily lift others up by expressing our belief that they can do anything they set their mind to, yet we keep ourselves small. It's often easy for us to see the potential in others but live in denial when it comes to our own potential. We may look at the celebrities of the world or people we look up to and think, "I can't do that." Well, maybe what they do is not in your wheelhouse, but what is? We are all placed on this earth with beautiful gifts to share with others. Not one of us is alike. How boring our world would be if everyone possessed the same strengths.

Many of us may believe that our career or job is where we need to make the most difference. I can tell you that what we do through our employment impacts others, but oftentimes what we do at home or in our community makes even more of a difference.

What we are most passionate about is where we truly shine the brightest. A great example is that of being a parent. I believe there is no greater gift than raising a child. If you are a stay-at-home parent, I hope you know that the time you are spending raising your children is invaluable. No job is more important.

Some of us have a difficult time believing that we make a positive impact on the world around us. We may have been raised with messages that cut down our self-esteem. Unfortunately, things we hear when we are young tend to follow us around like shadows. It takes work to block out the memories of hearing things such as, "You're not good enough, you won't amount to anything, you're not strong enough, you're too sensitive."

I'm grateful to have grown up with family who supported my dreams and pushed me toward them, but if you've experienced the opposite, it takes a great deal of strength and courage to reprogram your mind to think differently. I find that knowing who my tribe is and where I can go for support and encouragement makes a big difference. Being very careful to choose friends and family who will offer encouragement when you may be feeling down and discouraged is imperative. Having people you trust who will cheer you on is extremely important—especially when your ego is trying to shut you down out of fear.

Raise your hand if you've felt passionate about something but haven't ventured into that realm for fear of not being good enough. I'm guessing this is the majority of people. We often lack the confidence to move toward our dreams. Maybe we've had people question our dreams or tell us they aren't obtainable. Maybe we don't know where to start in fulfilling these dreams. Or maybe we are feeling a lack of confidence in our own abilities. Whatever the reason, I lovingly ask that you look at what you're missing out on by not stepping into things you feel passionate about. Often by holding back, we are keeping our own gifts hidden from the rest of the world.

As we discussed earlier, we each come into this world with our own gifts and talents which impact other lives. We don't always know the difference we make, but with every life we touch, hundreds of thousands are also impacted. The one person we touch creates a ripple effect. With that thought, can you imagine how sharing your gift or message with one person may help create small changes for so many?

Many years ago, a friend of mine asked me to be a part of an online magazine she planned to publish. My exact words were, "I can't write." We had many conversations back and forth during which I disagreed with her assessment of my abilities. She had seen some of my writing over the years and continued to insist that I was a talented writer. After much arm-twisting, I finally agreed to write articles for her magazine and found that I really enjoyed writing and felt inspired to continue. Again, it was a situation where I lacked belief in my own abilities which prevented me from doing anything further until someone in my life continued to push me.

Now, this definitely isn't the way it needs to be for any of us; however, if we are fortunate enough to have people who believe in our gifts and push us to share them, it often helps when we are standing in our own way. Over time it often gets easier to believe in our abilities, which is the ultimate goal. I heard from so many during that year when I helped with the online magazine who said my writing had impacted them in some way. Knowing I was making a difference inspired me to continue and find more ways to reach others. In reality, it should not matter if anyone else believes in us, but I think we all know that it certainly doesn't hurt to know others are standing on the sidelines rooting us on.

Reflection:

What gifts do you possess but have a hard time putting into action?

What, if anything, keeps you from believing in yourself and your gifts?

How would sharing your gifts impact others and the world?

_____
_____
_____
_____
_____
_____
_____
_____
_____
_____
_____
_____

BELIEVE IN YOU

We can pass through life holding back because we lack belief in our innate gifts, but not only do we hurt ourselves but we also keep our magnificence from others. Wouldn't you rather see what you are capable of during your lifetime? You never know what life you may change for the better, maybe even yours.

Be the Light

Can you relate to being like the lighthouse, always shining for others in the worst of storms? But what happens to the lighthouse during the storms? The waves batter the sides with force, sometimes causing damage to the structure over time.

Like the lighthouse, if we are constantly the light for others, it takes a toll over time on our own life. There needs to be balance between shining a light for others and shining it for ourselves. We can't let our well run dry because then we have nothing to keep us intact. Our purpose may be to shine light and love into the world but it has to start with us first. We must find ways to fill ourselves up so that we can present to others with a full tank.

In earlier chapters we talked about healing and specifically grief work. While this is important work, it's also important that once we release old emotions, thoughts, and grief, we in turn fill ourselves back up with positive, loving energy. If we engage in healing work, there has to be a balance between releasing and filling back up; otherwise, we leave a dark hole in our heart which is liable to fill up with anything coming its way. We want it to be filled up with strength, love, light, and self-worth, which may have been lacking previously. We want to move forward from a place of empowerment. This is what healing is all about.

When we feel empowered, we show up ready to shine our light for others to experience. We all know when walking down the street those people who we are attracted to because their whole aura feels bright, cheery, loving, and positive. These individuals are usually this way because they work on healing what hurts them and filling themselves back up with positive energy. They know that their purpose is to be a light for others, helping them to see. There is nothing more beautiful than seeing how your light impacts someone else and forms a ripple effect, touching hundreds of lives. As well as spreading healing throughout the world, this is part of your own healing.

How does one "be the light" in our sometimes dim world? As discussed previously, we first focus on our own light. To be bright for others, we first turn up our energy. Once we are full, we naturally emit an energy of light that shows in our smile, our voice, our eyes, our aura. We focus on ways to empower others. We listen without judgment. We give praise and grace to those around us. We allow others to be surrounded with our loving light, whatever they may be experiencing.

Sometimes all we can do is hold space for others who are suffering. We cannot take away their pain or change their experience, but we can be present in a loving way. Just our presence has the ability to change lives, either in a positive or negative way. Others may not remember your name or exactly what interaction they had with you, but they remember the way they felt in your presence. We want our energy to be remembered as enlightening, supportive, and loving.

In order to be this light, we focus on how we feel inside including our physical body, our heart energy, and our mind. Do you feel at peace? Do you feel empowered? Does your heart feel open? This energy is not something you can fake or pretend to embody. This energy is palpable. Each one of us has our own way of learning to embody this energy, but we must understand that once we find it, there is still effort that needs to take place. Just because for the past week we felt grounded, peaceful, open hearted, and bright doesn't mean that tomorrow it won't change.

I remember years ago feeling a little down and depressed. I no longer felt good about myself or my life. My heart felt closed. This was a significant change from how I felt the previous week. Someone said to me, "What did you stop doing that was helping you get into and stay in that good place previously?" *Aha, that's it.* I got comfortable with where I was and how I was feeling, so I had stopped doing the meditation, the exercise, and the self-care that had been paramount to getting me into that space of light for others to see.

It reminded me that our work is never done. We are constantly shifting, growing, and changing. Who we are today is different from who we were yesterday. In order to be a light for others, we must keep doing our own work and self-care. We need to take care of our own grief and healing. We need to focus on that which brings us peace, such as meditation, exercise, self-reflection, eating well, time with those we love, writing, or whatever helps us find our way back to our hearts. My way isn't the right way, it's just what I have found that works for me. I encourage you to find those practices or rituals which allow you to feel empowered and full of love and light.

Reflection:

Do you remember a time when your heart felt completely open? Journal about this experience.

What do you notice about your life when your light is shining bright?

What are your own gifts? How can you use them to help empower those around you?

_____
_____
_____
_____
_____
_____
_____
_____
_____
_____
_____
_____
_____

My light is a reflection of my own healing that I, in turn, shine to help others.

Final Thoughts

My wish is that you found my words to offer comfort, hope, support, and love. After reading my book I hope you realize you are not alone. The path to healing is not easy but it leads to beautiful places. I hope you can take something I wrote and create change in your own life. I wish for you to feel empowered, loved, worthy, and courageous as you navigate your life moving forward. May your journey be filled with peace, healing and love. Always remember to:

- Follow your dreams
- Be good to yourself
- Embrace your own healing and growth
- Find that which brings you joy
- Be the change
- Shine your light
- Spread Love
- Celebrate your magnificent self each and every day

With Love,

Dawn

Acknowledgments

To my son, Austin, the greatest gift of my life, thank you for your courage to follow your dreams, for it was in watching you that I became brave enough to follow mine. You are continually an inspiration in my life.

To my mom, Judy, thank you for always believing in me. Your constant love and support throughout my life have given me wings to fly places I never imagined.

To my partner, Ed, thank you for your unconditional love and support. These words would not have become a book without your encouragement. Thank you for having faith in me and pushing me to follow my passions.

To my furry child, Faith, thank you for allowing me to love you and provide you a home. Your support curled up next to my computer or sitting on my lap while writing provided a great deal of comfort and inspiration. May you now rest in peace knowing how much you are loved. And may your spirit always stay with me.

To those I love who are no longer on our physical plane but remain in spirit, thank you for helping me grow and become the person I am today. Your love stays close to my heart.

To my friend, writing coach, and publisher, Shanda, thank you for still believing in my abilities when I stopped believing in myself. Thank you for your gentle encouragement to get my words in print. I will forever be grateful.

About the Author

DAWN JACKSON is a registered nurse, grief specialist, author, and practitioner of multiple healing modalities.

Dawn resides in Sisters, Oregon, where she enjoys hiking and exploring the Pacific Northwest. Spending time in nature is where she fills herself up and finds peace during these turbulent times.

She's passionate about helping empower others to move from illness to wellness, from surviving to thriving. On this journey, she helps individuals recover from grief as a Certified Grief Recovery Specialist by teaching new tools and ways to work through loss.

Her own spiritual journey began over two decades ago after a painful divorce and the realization that she desired to find new ways to navigate life. While working on her own growth, she became passionate about passing on the gifts and wisdom she learned along the way. She enjoys working one-on-one with clients but is also passionate about writing. It's in writing that she gains clarity, insight, and peace, as she rediscovers her true self.

How to Get More Help

Throughout this book, I've talked to you about the importance of healing to create the life you desire and deserve. It took me many years of searching to find some concrete, effective ways to deal with things that hurt my heart. Although they all played a part in allowing me to live the life of my dreams, I cannot say enough about The Grief Recovery Method. This action-based method pushed me to move forward from the pain of my past in ways that no other workshop, training, or therapy had been able to accomplish.

I invite you to visit my website, www.dawnmichelejackson.com, for more information or to schedule a call with me.